Tea 〳 〵 〳 Northwest

Featuring Tea Rooms,
Tea Events,
and Tea Time Recipes

Sharron and John deMontigny

J&S Publishing
Corvallis, Oregon USA

The Tea Cup Graphics in this publication are
the property of Pat's Web Graphics. Other
photos are from the private albums of J&S
Publishing and/or were provided by Tea
Room proprietors.

Cover photo and design
by John deMontigny

Also by Sharron and John deMontigny
Tea Time Journal - ISBN 0-9741814-0-4
Tea Rooms Northwest 1st edition - ISBN 0-9741814-1-2
Tea Rooms Northwest 2nd edition - ISBN 0-9741814-2-0

J&S Publishing
2397 N.W. Kings Blvd. # 148
Corvallis, Oregon 97330 USA
Telephone: 541-753-1502.
E-Mail: *TeaRoomsNorthwest@hotmail.com*

Tea Rooms Northwest 3rd edition
ISBN # 978-0-9741814-3-1

Printed in the United States of America

J&S Publishing

About the Authors

John and Sharron reside in Corvallis, Oregon, a college town midway between the mountains and the ocean. Yes, they are avid Oregon State University Beaver fans!

John was born in Quebec, Canada, and moved to the United States when he was five, settling first on the East Coast. He eventually moved with his family to California, where he was raised. After high school, he enlisted in the U.S. Air Force, where he served for twenty-five years. After retirement in 1991, John went to work for the Hewlett Packard Co., where he is still employed.

Sharron was born and raised in San Francisco, California and is proud to call herself a "fourth generation San Franciscan." She met John during the summer of 1963 and they were married in 1968, at which time she became a military wife. While raising their three children in California and Oregon, she owned a catering business. Upon their move to Corvallis in 1990, she gave up the business and became a cook for the men of Tau Kappa Epsilon Fraternity, whom she calls her "other family."

John and Sharron are also the proud grandparents of

 four boys and four girls. Fortunately, they all live nearby and they are able to visit them often. The grandkids are also wonderful tea companions.

About the Cover Photo

*This year, we thought it would be fun to produce
our own cover. We hope that the end result is
pleasing to the eye and that it conveys the message
that we are trying to share ... Tea Time can be
filled with sentiment and it is always special. The
gold tea pot was a gift to Sharron and the tea cup
is one she picked up while on one of her many
treasure hunts to antiques and collectable shops.
The creamer and sugar bowl, as well as the china,
were borrowed from daughter Alicia. The china
was passed down to Alicia from her grandmother
Charlotte deMontigny. Sharron's mom, O'Day
Tynan Robertson, again graces the cover, as do
Sharron's '60's gloves and pearls. Finally, the large
round crocheted doily is one Sharron won a few
years ago. All are special treasures!*

Acknowledgments

We would like to thank the many people who took the time to contact us during the past three years. It was with their help that we were able to keep abreast of the many changes in Northwest tea rooms. Because of them, there are many new tea rooms listed in this third edition of *Tea Rooms Northwest.*

Many thanks go out to Jan Komar for the many hours she spent proof-reading our book, and to Irene Gresick, who continues to share her publishing expertise with us.

Last, but certainly not least, we want to acknowledge all of the tea room proprietors who returned our questionnaire, took our many phone calls, responded to our e-mails, shared favorite recipes, welcomed us to their tea rooms and in every way helped us complete this labor of love. We hope that we are representing them in a manner that pleases and benefits them.

Thanks

Dedications

Again we dedicate this book to our wonderful family:
Stephen and Jennifer deMontigny, Todd and Alicia
Jacob and Deanna Reisdorf, with loving appreciation
for all their support and assistance during the writing
of this book. We also dedicate it to our grandchildren
Brandon, Ashley, Jason, Christian, Jessica, Daphne,
Hannah and Marcus, who have added joy to our lives
in so many ways

We especially dedicate it to all the tea room owners
who gave us the basis for this book. Without them,
there would be no book.

Tea with the Grandkids

Brandon

Ashley

Jason at Myrtle's
Tea Room

Christian at
Myrtle's Tea Room

Jessica at Lisa's
Tea Room

Daphne at Althea's
Tea Room

Hannah at a Sister
Act Tea

Marcus at Lisa's
Tea Room

Disclaimers

We made a sincere effort to find and include *ALL* the tearooms in the Northwest. How-ever, we know that some are missing from this book. If you are a tea room owner, or if you have a favorite tea room that is not in this guide, please let us know. We have added some tea rooms in Northern California where you can expand your adventures. The tea rooms in Canada have been deleted due to our inability to keep in close contact with them and the difficulty of marketing our book in Canada. You can still find them in our 2nd edition, but be sure to call first before visiting them.

Our quarterly newsletter will update this guide on a regular basis along with information on tea events of interest. Simply subscribe by emailing us at TeaRoomsNorthwest@hotmail.com.

Everything is subject to change! To the best of our knowledge, the information we have included in this guide was accurate at the time of publication. Tea rooms may change their *prices*, days and hours of operation, location and menu offerings. Unfortunately, they also close or discontinue offering tea. We highly recommend that you **call ahead before venturing out** and remember … many tea rooms *require reservations*!

The path to heaven passes through a teapot.

Ancient Proverb

Tea is wealth itself, because there is nothing that can not be lost, no problem that will not disappear, no problem that will not float away, between the first sip and the last.

The Minister of Leaves

TABLE OF CONTENTS

Promoting the Love of Tea

We cannot believe that we are publishing the *3rd edition* of our book, *Tea Rooms Northwest*. I guess that when you are associated with such a wonderful industry, time just passes quickly. Between tea room visits, enjoying home teas and reading everything I can get my hands on that is related to tea, I have been pretty busy since publishing our second edition.

John and I made some special *tea time memories* when we took a cruise to Eastern Canada and New England. One of the highlights was taking tea at Chateau Frontanec in Quebec City. It is amazing to enjoy tea at a location you never even thought you would visit! Two days later we were taking tea at The Citadel in Nova Scotia. That was also a most memorable experience where tea was presented in one of the buildings that housed the former galley and dining room at this historic site.

I had the pleasure of attending the first "An Occasion for Tea" in Salt Lake City and will be sure to make as many of those as I possibly can. It was fabulous and I loved being surrounded by other lovers of tea.

We enjoyed a special "Tea at Sea" Cruise with Cyrilla Gleason, Susan Springer and a group of new found friends. I will go anywhere to take tea!

We do not consider ourselves tea experts. We have just had the opportunity to take tea in many tea rooms and enjoy writing about our experiences. We are neither endorsing nor critiquing these tea rooms; we are just sharing them with you. Our intent is to encourage you to seek out tea rooms and to enjoy all that they have to offer....peace, tranquility, great tea and delicious food. Go with an open mind knowing that all tea rooms are different.

Remember that prices, hours, locations, etc., change. Unfortunately, tearooms occasionally close, but, happily, others open. Today's economy is affecting everyone so some tea rooms have changed their days and hours. Be sure to call before heading out so you are not disappointed.

Some tea rooms are not wheelchair accessible, which is usually due to their historic designation.

You may subscribe to our quarterly emailed newsletter for regularly updated information. Please feel free to call or email us for information and updates.

Phone: 541-753-1502
e-mail: TeaRoomsNorthwest@hotmail.com

Happy Tea Times!

Sharron

The Origin of Tea Time

In the early 1800s in England, dinner was usually served quite late at night. It is said that Anna, the Duchess of Bedford, started having hunger pangs while awaiting the evening meal, which was often served around 9 p.m. She requested that a tray of bread and butter, along with a pot of tea, be sent to her room. Soon, along with the tea and bread, dainty pastries with clotted cream and preserves were added. It then became the custom for her to invite some society ladies to join her and "tea time" came into being. Though originally intended to be an evening snack, it is now what many of us think of as Afternoon Tea, and it is served anywhere between 11 a.m. and 4 p.m. The other wording for afternoon tea was low tea, as it was served at a low table, much like our modern coffee table.

High Tea was actually the evening meal of the common people, and it was served at the dinner table, or high table. Served around 6 p.m., High Tea consisted of trays of meats, cheeses, fish or eggs along with bread and butter, cake and tea. Side dishes were often added to the meal. Today, many tea rooms serve a Ploughman's Plate, which is similar to the traditional high tea.

It seems that one was more suited to women and the other to men. One was a diversion and the other a meal for the working man!

Theme Teas

One of the most enjoyable ways to enjoy tea with friends is to hostess a theme tea. I am including some suggestions which are easy and fun ... and anyone can do them! For colored bread, order your bread from a bakery and request your desired color.

Seasonal decorations may be used to adorn your table, and napkins and tablecloths in the appropriate colors complete the theme. Individual favors which match the theme are always a nice touch.

Easter Tea

Mimosa's
Hot cross buns
Deviled eggs
Stuffed cherry tomatoes
Carrot and walnut sandwiches
Ham salad spirals
Pineapple cream cheese sandwiches open-faced
Carrot cake
Easter egg cookies
Macaroons

4th of July Tea

Lemonade
Iced Tea
Strawberry/blueberry scones
Ambrosia
Tomato on crostini
Strawberry cream cheese sandwiches
Chicken and almond sandwiches
Cucumber with cherry tomato topping
Mini shortcakes
Lemon cookies
Blueberry bread

Scottish Tea

Scottish Breakfast Tea
Cheese scones
Scotch eggs
Cheddar with egg salad sandwiches
Smoked salmon and cream cheese open faced
Cucumber sandwiches
Beef and horseradish on toasted bread fingers
Chocolate shortbread
Walnut and coconut cookies
Lemon tarts

Garden Tea

Iced mixed fruit tea
Savory scones
Mixed berry fruit cup
Ham wrapped asparagus
Ants on a log
Shredded carrot and olive on white bread
Open faced cucumber rounds
Chopped beets and cream cheese sandwiches
Orange chiffon cake
Flower shaped cookies
Cream cheese stuffed strawberries

Christmas Tea

Orange spiced tea
Hot fruit compote
Cranberry scones
Cream cheese stuffed dates
Roast beef with horseradish sandwiches
Turkey ranch wraps
Ham biscuits
Fruitcake
Chocolate fudge bites
Christmas tree iced cookies

Brewing Tips

Always start with cold water.
Heat your teapot with warm water.
Add one teaspoon of tea leaves per cup
(a heaping teaspoon for iced).
Do not over-boil the water.

Black Teas

Bring water to a boil and remove from heat. Add tea and steep for 5 minutes. If you like a stronger, pungent cup of tea, add a bit more tea. Steeping longer than 5 minutes may produce a bitter tea. Add hot water if tea is too strong.

Green and Pouchong Teas

Bring water to a pre-boil and remove from heat. Add tea and steep up to 3 minutes. Longer steeping will cause tea to be bitter. Quality green teas can be steeped more than once.

Oolong and White Teas

Bring water to a pre-boil. Add tea and steep 4-6 minutes. Oolongs can vary in steeping time, so taste to test. They can be re-steeped several times.

Tisanes (Herbals)

Bring water to a rolling boil. Add herbs, one heaping teaspoon per cup (for iced herbals, add one Tbsp.). Steep 5-9 minutes. Herbs will not get bitter if left longer.

Rooibos

Bring water to a full boil. Pour over tea leaves and steep for 5-7 minutes. Since this is not a true tea, steeping longer will not produce a bitter tea.

Welcome

to

Oregon

A La Fontaine

Vintage Day Spa & Tea Room
1708 Springhill Drive N.W.
Albany, Oregon 97321
541-928-0747
800-531-4306
www.alafontaine.com

From I-5, follow signs for Civic Center Albany/Hwy 20 Corvallis. Cross the Willamette River Bridge in right hand lane. Take immediate right on Springhill Drive and go just over a mile. After the Quarry-Nebergall intersection sign, turn left at brick pillars with white lanterns.

More than a tea room, A La Fontaine offers a recipe for relaxation along with afternoon tea. The garden-style, turn of the century tea room, is done in yellow with black French toile accents. French doors open to a billowy, curtained, private, garden room which features a demitasse tea tasting bar. There are several outdoor settings which Linda uses during the summer - patio, veranda, lawn and garden.

The Full Afternoon Tea consists of scone or crumpet, crème fraichê, lemon curd, fruit, a variety of tea sandwiches, wrap or quiche, crackers and cheese and dessert for $24.99. This tea is offered to groups of four or more and for special events only. This would be a great location to hold a birthday, anniversary, shower or corporate meeting. The proprietor will work with food allergies and special diets, and offer whole foods/organic whenever possible.

Doll collectors may want to gather for tea since another business, L.B. Designs, a doll sculpting studio and school, is located on the premises.

Linda offers a spa menu that features everything from massages and facials to mineral soaks and a quiet room. A Spa Plate can be added to any spa session and it includes an arrangement of fruit, cheese and crackers, sandwich, vegetables, and dessert for $15.

Treat yourself to a special day at Touch of Class Day Spa.

MC/V/Checks
Wheelchair Accessible
Off-Street Parking

Open Tuesday through Saturday. Spa treatments are by appointment. Tea time is by reservation 2 weeks in advance. Cancellation notice required.

Proprietors
Autograph_____Date_____

Afternoon Tea by Stephanie

508 S.E. 9th Avenue
Canby, Oregon 97013
503-266-7612

Owner Stephanie Allen is an instructor for tea and etiquette. Her presentations are at various locations in the Northwest.

Stephanie does presentations for women, For the Love of Teacups and Silver, Enriching Our Lives, as well as, workshops for youth, which are age specific. One class which is offered is Etiquette for Youth for 8 to 12 year olds, which ends with a tea party. The Dining with Style for Teens includes a three-course dinner to practice their new skills. For the 4 to 7 year olds, there are Imaginary Tea Parties complete with tea sets, hats and gloves. These classes are taught at various locations including the Historic Deepwood Estate in Salem and Carnegie Center in Oregon City. Special dietary needs can be accommodated with advance notice.

Stephanie retails Simpson and Vale teas, along with her special tea accessories, at Deepwood Estate and Carnegie Center.

She is making plans to offer traditional teas in the near future.

MC/V/and Checks Accepted

For dates and times of workshops, or to schedule your own, contact Stephanie directly.

Proprietors
Autograph_____Date_____

Albertina's

Albertina Kerr Center

424 N.E. 22nd Avenue
Portland, Oregon 97232
503-231-3909 / 503-231-0216
www.albertinakerr.org

They are located near Lloyd Center and Oregon Convention Center close to the intersection of Sandy Boulevard and 20th.

The house that has become The Shops at Albertina Kerr has a long and interesting history. Located on land that was donated by Alexander Kerr, founder of the Kerr Jar Manufacturing Co., it became a care center for children in 1921. The nursery closed in 1967 then re-opened in 1981 as the Old Kerr Nursery, housing the present volunteer-staffed Shops at Albertina Kerr. Some of the current programs which benefit from the shops include foster care for children with special needs, early intervention programs, psychiatric residential services, group home and supportive-living services for people with developmental disabilities and more. The businesses which comprise The Shops at Albertina Kerr include a gift shop, antiques shop, thrift shop and Albertina's, which offers luncheons and catering.

Though primarily a luncheon restaurant, Albertina's is described as having a "tea room" atmosphere. Once or twice a year that atmosphere becomes a reality when a Valentine's Tea and Summer Garden Tea are offered at a cost of $25. A sample menu consists of ribbon tea sandwiches, chive and egg pinwheels, chicken-almond fingers, lemon tartlets, fudge party bars, chocolate-dipped strawberries, sugared grapes and tea or coffee. Sherry and wine may be purchased at an additional cost.

This would be a wonderful opportunity to take tea in a very special setting while helping out this very worthwhile organization. Mark your calendar now so you don't forget about this very special event!

The property is available to rent for special events and there is an in-house caterer.

MC/V/Checks
Wheelchair Accessible
Lot and Street Parking

Luncheon seatings are 11:30 and 1, Monday through Friday. Reservations are recommended. They offer an annual Valentine's Tea and a Garden Tea in July.

Proprietors
Autograph_____Date_____

Althea's Tea Room

184 S.E. Oak Street
Dallas, Oregon 97338
503-831-4777
altheastr@qwest.net

Heading west from Salem on Hwy 22, follow signs to Dallas. Once in Dallas, at the second signal keep to the left onto Main Street. Continue to Oak Street and turn left. The tea room is on the left-hand side at the end of the block.

Now celebrating her fifth year in business, Patricia, along with her daughter Frances, continues to offer a warm and friendly place to take afternoon tea. I am sure her mother, for whom the tea room is named, is beaming with pride.

Situated in an interesting older building in the downtown area, Althea's offers three rooms for your "tea sipping" pleasure. All of the rooms feature large lace-covered windows, tables decked out in floral-patterned tablecloths and cloth napkins, and white "doilies" at each place setting. Customers select their cup and saucer from one of the antique cabinets which are situated in the two main rooms. The tea pots are wrapped in pretty cozies and the tea sets are presented on tiered servers.

There are three tea sets to choose from. The first is Dena's Tea, which consists of tea sandwiches, fresh fruit, assorted sweets and a delicious scone with clotted cream, lemon curd and strawberry jam for $11.50. The other two selections are Hanna's Tea, which is scones and tea for $6.50 and Bethany's Tea, which is tea sandwiches, cheese selection, seasonal fruit, savories, assorted sweets, scones with all the trimmings and a pot of tea for $16.50.

Lunch items are available and may include soup or quiche of the day, sandwiches, or Fran's Pear Salad. Specialty desserts are featured, as well as coffee, lemonade and iced tea. Theme and holiday teas are offered throughout the year. Groups are welcome with advance arrangements. Pat also offers Brunch on the 1st Saturday of the month from 10-2 for $13.95.

There is a selection of gifts available for purchase as well as the loose leaf tea that is served in the tea room.

MC/V/Checks
Wheelchair Accessible
Free Street Parking

The tea room is open Tuesday through Saturday 10-3, and Monday 11-2:30. Lunch is served 11-2. The last seating for tea is 2 p.m. Tea reservations are required 24-hours in advance for more then 4 people and are recommended for all others. Tea and scones are served all day.

Proprietors
Autograph_____Date_____

23

Amelia's Antiques

370 River Road
Eugene, Oregon 97404
541-688-3900
1-877-1058
amelias2000@aol.com

Take Hwy 126 or Hwy 105 to Downtown Eugene. Go right on 6th Street to Chambers. Take Chambers 2 blocks. After the railroad overpass you will see the tea room on the left side of the road. Watch for a flag and a red and black sign. The nearest cross streets are Briarcliff and Crocker.

This tea room, which was voted "Best of Tearooms 2006" by the Register Guard, is located in the Historic Johansen-Moody Home and is listed on the historic register. One can easily imagine the lady of the house serving tea here in 1899, shortly after the house was built. Kathi offer tea for up to 20 guests in what she calls a "country vintage" ambience. Weather permitting, tea is also offered in the garden under the lilacs. The tea tables are covered with vintage linens and napkins, and the tables and table service are also vintage.

The first tea offers 2 scones with Devonshire cream and jam or a dessert choice for $3.95. A small pot of tea is an additional $3 per person. The Duchess Tea includes warm scones, assorted sandwiches, fancy tea desserts and a pot of tea or coffee for $14.95. And finally, the Queen's High Tea, which is priced at $19.50 per person, includes warm scones, finger sandwiches, soup, fruit compote, assorted tea desserts and bottomless tea.

For lunch one might select soup and/or sandwich or the entrée of the week, and these items range in price from $5.50 to $10.50. Vegetarian is offered daily. The tea choices are numerous and may be served iced during the summer. Kathi calls her tea room comfortable and cozy, and she says they treat everyone like family. That's a wonderful environment in which to enjoy a leisurely afternoon tea.

MC/V/DEB/Checks
Not Wheelchair Accessible
On-Street and Limited Lot Parking
Carpooling Recommended

The shop is open Tuesday through Saturday from 10 to 5 and Sunday 12 to 4. Tea is offered from 11 to 4 Tuesday through Saturday. The last tea is served at 4 p.m. Reservations for groups of 6 or more must be made 2 days in advance. Reservations are also required for theme teas.

Proprietors
Autograph_____Date_____

The ANZAC Tea Parlour

218 W. 4th Street
The Dalles, Oregon 97058
541-296-5877
eagy@gorge.net
www.anzactea.com

Take I-84 eastbound to exit 84. Continue to Liberty Street, turn right. Turn right again on 4th Street. The tea parlor is on the left. I-84 westbound, take the downtown exit, continue to Liberty. Turn left, go 2 blocks and turn right on 4th Street. The tea parlor is on the left near Saint Peter's Landmark Church.

Opened in 2004 by Bev and Alan Eagy, this tea room's name stands for Australian-New Zealand Army Corps. Located in the historic 1865 home of Northwest cattle king Ben Snipes, the ambience is an Australian tea parlour in an historic setting. Bev lived in Australia for 20 years and says, "she brought a taste of Australia to the beautiful Columbia River Gorge."

A bit if interesting information … Aussies call cookies "biscuits." The famous ANZAC biscuits are crisp cookies made for the ANZAC soldiers during WWI. Bev imports Australian Golden syrup to make authentic ANZAC biscuits

There are over 100 varieties of tea to choose from. A full lunch menu is available, from homemade soups or Crumpets & Tea, to hearty Aussie Meat Pie. The 3-course "Australian Romance" High Tea, which is offered for $18.95, includes chicken almond and cucumber sandwiches, olive roll, sun-dried tomato quiche, petite ANZAC biscuits, chocolate-dipped strawberry, an Australian cream scone, blackberry scone and dark chocolate scone with Devonshire cream and jams, and a special dessert. Fresh-baked desserts are available each day! The dessert menu includes Crème Brulee, Pavlova, Tiramisu, Three-berry Cheesecake and Rice Pudding. The full lunch menu and tea selections can be viewed at www.anzactea.com

There is a take-away menu, and catering is available. There are a variety of teapots, teacups, vintage hats, teapot jewelry and other gifts to choose from. Bev also makes beautiful wedding cakes, many of which are featured on the website. Walk-ins welcome, reservations appreciated.

Checks/Cash
Wheelchair Accessible
Free Street Parking

Hours of operation are Tuesday through Saturday 11 to 4.

Proprietors
Autograph_____Date_____

Berry Sweet Tea Parties

4795 S.W. Watson Avenue
Beaverton, Oregon 97005
503-989-7572
julie@berrysweetparties.com / www.berrysweetparties.com

From I-5, take 217 N (exit 292). Take exit A (Beaverton-Hillsdale/Canyon Road). Go left on Hwy 10/Beaverton-Hillsdale Hwy. Take a left on S.W. Watson Avenue and proceed 3 blocks to the corner of S.W. Watson and S.W. 3rd.

Julie Berry opened her tea room, which is located in a 1900's house in Old Towne Beaverton, in 2006. She does tea parties by reservation for groups of 6 to 12 people. For the ladies, the tea room transforms them back to vintage times where elegance, quaint atmosphere and dainty treats are the perfect setting for any group. At Berry Sweet tea parties, your child can play dress up, drink tea, eat treats and even learn the importance of the lost art of proper etiquette through fun and games. Packages are available for your upcoming event - birthday party, wedding and baby showers, book clubs, Red Hat Society meetings, garden clubs scrapbook clubs, and any other gathering looking for a special event. For larger parties, at home catering services are available.

There are three children's packages, each 1 ½ hours long, to choose from. The first, priced at $15 each, is the Cupcake Party which includes scones & breads, fresh fruit, gourmet cupcakes and lemonade. Next is the Berry Sweet Tea Party which offers scones & bread, fresh fruit, finger sandwiches, gourmet cupcakes and lemonade for $20 per person. The final children's tea is the Princess Party which is priced at $25 per person. The menu is scones & breads, fresh fruit, finger sandwiches, gourmet cupcakes and pink lemonade. Each "princess" receives a tiara and wand to wear and to take home. All of the children's parties include 2 pre-arranged games, tea history and etiquette lessons and the use of dress up "accessories."

For adults there are two teas. The Tea & Tarts Party offers assorted scones & breads, a variety of tarts and fresh fruit for $15. Priced at $20, the High Tea includes finger sandwiches, fruit and assorted desserts. Both teas include a selection of gourmet loose leaf teas.

If you wish to rent the room, it is available for $12 per person for two hours. You may bring your favorite dessert and the beverages will be provided. A party assistant will help with treats and clean up.

Party add-ons, such as invitations, flowers, balloons and corsages are available for purchase also. For more details and to arrange your special event, contact Julie at the above number.

Checks/Cash
Not Handicapped Accessible
On Street Parking

Tea is by reservation only.

Proprietors
Autograph_____Date_____

Blue Angel Heavenly Delectables

10500 S.E. 26th # A33
Milwaukie, Oregon 97222
503-975-9744
blueangelbake@yahoo.com

Teas are on-location and the place is to be determined at time of booking.

Elise Hamilton offers private teas only, either at your location of choice or at the historic Broetje House in Milwaukie. Built in 1889, the home offers the perfect ambience for your special tea. The banquet room can seat up to 150 people and is available for weddings, retirements, birthdays and other events.

Blue Angel Custom Bakery uses only the freshest, highest quality, natural ingredients to prepare your unique menu. Many of the recipes are one of a kind and each menu is made to order. The tea menu offers tea and scones or Afternoon Tea up to a High Tea package. All teas include scones and there is a list of 74 to choose from. Dessert is included in High Tea only but may be added to the other teas at nominal cost per person. Tea Zone is the house tea and coffee is available upon request.

Some of the tea choices include entrée soup or salad and the selection is extensive. Elise encourages you to make your event unique by offering you some basic packages to which you may add selected items. All packages include a choice of Premium Exotic Tea.

Specialty items are a tart, pastries and an old family recipe for potato cheese enchiritos. As for dessert ... just reading the list was a pleasure! There are bars, tortes, tarts, crisps, cakes, cookies, breads and muffins. Where to begin?

MC/V/Checks
Wheelchair Accessible at Broetje House
Large Parking Lot at Broetje House

Tea is by reservation only. A 50% non-refundable deposit is required at time of booking. Call for further information.

Proprietors
Autograph_____Date_____

Historic Broetje House

3101 S.E. Courtney Road
Milwaukie, Oregon 97222
503-659-8860
thebroetjehouse@aol.com
www.thebroetjehouse.com

From I-205, take exit 11. Turn left and go to the second stop light. Turn right onto Oatfield Road. Travel 3½ miles and you will see Broetje House on the left.

Lorraine and Lois offer teas in the Historic Broetje House, a Queen Anne farm house, circa 1889. The original house has retained its historic elegance while a special-events facility has been added adjacent to the house. The two buildings are connected by a lovely glass and tiled breezeway, which offers a view of the beautifully manicured lawn and lovely gardens.

Teas may be arranged for groups of up to 80 people. A typical tea for 25 people would be $25 per person, which would meet the $475 minimum. This is a three-course tea and it includes tea, assorted tea sandwiches, fresh fruit, scones, and desserts. A tea and desserts event would have a $250 minimum. There is an assortment of tea labels to choose from to accompany your tea set. Coffee is also available.

If you are interested in booking a luncheon or dinner event, there is an extensive menu from which to choose. Groups of up to 150 can be accommodated. The location is also perfect for weddings, either inside by the fireplace or outside by the gazebo. Check their website for more details.

MC/V/AE/Checks
Wheelchair Accessible
Parking Lot

Teas are served by reservation with a two week notice. They are served Monday through Friday only.

Proprietors
Autograph_____Date_____

The Campbell House Inn

Inn & Restaurant

252 Pearl Street
Eugene, Oregon 97401
541-343-1119
campbellhouse@campbellhouse.com / www.campbellhouse.com

From I-5, take exit 194B onto I-105 then take the Coburg/Downtown exit. Stay left and follow City Center/Mall signs. Cross river, turn right at 2nd exit (Downtown/Hult Center-Hwy 126). Make an immediate right at the signal onto High Street. Turn left on 5th Avenue then turn right on to Pearl Street. You will see the Inn on the left side of the street. Pull into the drive at the sign and enter the large parking lot.

This lovely bed and breakfast is located at the foot of Skinners Butte, within walking distance to 5th Street Market and other spots of interest. An expansive Victorian House situated on a hillside, it immediately impressed you as you drive up to it. More delights await you upon entering. Beautiful antiques and room décor are featured in the 20 guestrooms as well as the charming public rooms. The lobby features a gift nook which offers sweatshirts, birdhouses, CDs, cards and more.

Event teas (Mother's Day and Christmas Holiday Season) begin with a sipped soup, followed by scones with jam and cream. The last two courses are served together on a tiered server and consist of three types of finger sandwiches and assorted desserts, which may be apricot truffles, cream puffs, fruit tarts, shortbread or a chocolate truffle. Tea is poured by charming and friendly servers, who also offer additional sandwiches. Other beverages are available upon request. The cost of the tea is $34 per person, and the Christmas teas may includes carolers or a roving storyteller for entertainment.

Children's teas may be scheduled as private parties during the year at a cost of $18 per child, plus a room charge, with special character themes such as American Girl or Harry Potter.

Dinner is now served in the Inn nightly from 6-9 p.m., with entrees ranging in price from $12-$31 featuring Northwest cuisine. Soups, salads, appetizers and desserts are also offered, as well as a Prix Fixe Menu. Special diets may be accommodated.

MC/V/DIS/AV/DEB/Check
Wheelchair Accessible
Lot Parking

Special teas are offered during the year including Mother's Day weekend and on specific weekends during December. Reservations are required. Private teas may be arranged. Call for information regarding groups.

Proprietors
Autograph_____Date_____

The Charms of Tea

Tea Room & Cafe

333 First Avenue W.
Albany, Oregon 97321
541-928-9475
www.nowtowns.com/aromatique/charmsoftea

From I-5, take the Albany exit. Follow the signs to Hwy 20 (Corvallis/Albany City Center). Turn left on 1st Avenue and go 2½ blocks. The Charms of Tea is on the right-hand side, across from the Wells Fargo parking lot.

"Charm" certainly describes Shannon Miller's shabby chic and slightly retro tea room. The tea room is nestled in the back of Aromatique, a beautiful boutique that invites you to slow down the minute you walk in the door. As you enter the tea room, you are greeted with twinkling lights, the sound of fountains and lovely soft music. The tables are covered in black and white cloths and there are accents of red throughout the room. In the back of the room, there is a living room setting with a couch and chairs which are centered around a cozy fireplace. You are invited to take in and enjoy the beautiful surroundings and cozy ambience, where Shannon takes you back to when life was much slower-paced. She asks you to "relax, listen to music, smell the aromas and visit with your friends."

There are 5 tea sets to choose from: the Poet's Tea offers soup, salad and a scone for $10.50 and the Red Letter Tea which includes soup, 3 finger sandwiches and a scone is also $10.50 For more substantial teas, choose from the Empress Tea of sorbet, 3 finger sandwiches, a scone, 2 savories and a dessert for $14.50 or the Regal Tea which includes sorbet, soup, 3 tea sandwiches, 2 savories, a scone and a decadent dessert for $16.50. If you prefer, you may choose the Scone-Lover Tea which is the same as the Regal Tea but offers 2 scones and no dessert for $16.50. All include a pot of tea. If you prefer, there is a lunch menu to select from as well - Greek or turkey panini sandwiches or grilled portabello mushroom sandwich. There is also a ginger Asian salad, eggplant casserole or two soups to choose from. Coffee is available upon request and special dietary needs can be accommodated.

Aromatique sells body care products as well as books, cards, tea accessories and a large selection of over 60 loose teas.

MC/V/DEB/Checks
Wheelchair Accessible
Lot & Free Street Parking

The tea room is open Friday and Saturday 11-3. Reservations required for 4 or more. 24 hour reservations confirmation required. Groups can make arrangement for tea on any day.

Proprietors
Autograph_____Date_____

Cheryl's Cup of Tea

1109 Monroe Street
Oregon City, Oregon 97045
503-655-1521
cheryl@cherylscupoftea.com
www.cherylscupoftea.com

From McLoughlin (99E) northbound, go right at 14th Street (signal) then 1 block to Main. Turn right on Main then left on 12th Street (go under railway trestle). Go to stop sign, cross over Washington Street and follow 12th to Monroe. Turn right-the house is on the right. From southbound, take McLoughlin to 14th, turn left and follow above directions. From I-205 take exit 9 and go to 99E. Follow above directions.

The new location of Cheryl's tea room is a small 1900 English style cottage that presents a charming view of the Willamette River and West Linn Hill. The house also has a wrap around deck that offers a view of the surrounding hillsides. There are three rooms awaiting your visit. Each is decorated in an English garden theme complete with lace, linens and flowers. Retail items, including tea and tea accoutrements, are offered for sale. Most of them are one of a kind.

Many of the menu choices will be those offered at the previous location – delicious quiche, veggie sandwich, soup & salad, and luncheon sandwiches. The tea sets start with Jackie's "Jammin" Scone which is served with table cream, lemon curd and fruit for $6.50. Debbie's Delectable Dessert offers a choice of cake, pie, trifle or other Dessert of the Day for $5. Nancy's Nibbler Plate has finger sandwiches and three tea cookies for $8. Finally, Mother Marie's Mouthwatering Full Tea, which requires reservations. This tea includes scones with table cream, lemon curd and jams, assorted tea sandwiches and mini quiche, homemade soup or salad and dessert tray for $17. All of the above teas include a pot of tea. Gratuity is not included in the prices. Whether you are in the mood for tea foods or a good sandwich, Cheryl can tailor the menu to accommodate individual needs.

Cash/Checks
Debit and Credit cards will be added
Wheelchair Accessible
Free Street and Private Parking

Tea is by private appointment only. Special events will be posted on their website. Groups of 4 to 35 can be accommodated. 3 day advance reservations. 48 hour cancellation required.

Proprietors
Autograph_____Date_____

Columbia Gorge Hotel

4000 Westcliff Drive
Hood River, Oregon 97031
541-386-5566 / 800-345-1921
cghotel@gorge.net
www.ColumbiaGorgeHotel.com

Take I-84 east from Portland to Exit 62 and follow the signs. Cross the freeway and the hotel is on the left. It is one hour east of Portland.

How nice it is to see another fine hotel offering afternoon tea. Time was when all the big resort and city hotels offered tea, but unfortunately many have ceased that tradition. This beautiful hotel, built in 1921, is referred to as a "Romantic Jazz-Age Hotel" and it is a national landmark. After your relaxing tea time, take a leisurely walk around the hotel and take in all the beauty she has to offer, both inside and out.

Tea is served in the lovely dining room overlooking the grounds of the hotel. White linens, vintage china cups and saucers, sparkling crystal and fresh flowers grace the tables. The buffet table is an elegant presentation with beautiful silver servers and other tea accoutrements. The high tea consists of assorted Columbia Gorge Hotel specialty tea sandwiches and savories-smoked salmon roulade, cucumber sandwich, beef Wellington puff pastry, plantation pecan & chicken salad sandwich, brie & brio tarts, and ham with mushroom/olive panini. The buffet also includes scones and biscuits, fruit tartlets, chocolate nut clusters, chocolate dipped strawberries, cookies and shortbread. Tea is poured at your table from vintage teapots, and the cost for all of this is only $20 per person. What a wonderful way to treat yourself to something special!

Brunch, lunch, dinner and appetizers are offered in other areas of the hotel and there is a gift shop for browsing and shopping.

Besides taking tea at the Columbia Gorge Hotel, you might want to add a weekend stay at this fabulous hotel! Their breakfast and dinner offerings are also wonderful and the rooms are quite elegant!!

MC/V/DIS
Wheelchair Accessible
Lot Parking

This historic property is for sale. Call before going!

Proprietors
Autograph_____Date_____

Country Cottage Bakery & Tearoom

205 Fern Valley Road
Phoenix, Oregon 97353
541-535-5113
mlawrenceJR@chater.net

From I-5, take exit 24; look for The Shoppes on the west side of highway. Country Cottage is located at the far end of The Shoppes on the left.

The decor, designed by David Linderman, is enchanting. With picket fences on the windows, a trellis in the dining area and floor-to-ceiling murals depicting outdoor scenes, the room has a true garden feel. What a charming place to take afternoon tea.

High Tea offers assorted finger sandwiches, brown sugar shortbread, blackberry and strawberry scones, assorted desserts, fresh fruit, hot tea or beverage of choice for $15.95 per person. Pastries and muffins are offered for $1.50 to $2.95 and include scones, cinnamon rolls, pumpkin or bran muffins, bear claws or Danish and cookies (chocolate chip, peanut butter or oatmeal). If you desire dessert only, the bakery case is laden with wonderful temptations - chocolate cake, carrot cake, cheesecakes, cream pie, tiramisu, brownies and lemon bars. Assorted beverages, priced at $1.95, can be purchased to accompany any of the above treats. Personally, I recommend the iced Paradise Tea!

After your afternoon tea, stop at the bakery and select something special to enjoy later in the evening. Or perhaps you will be interested in something really yummy for breakfast the next day!

There is a gift shop and outside catering is offered.

V/MC/AE/DEB
Wheelchair Accessible
Lot Parking

Afternoon Tea is served Tuesday through Friday from 11 to 3 by reservation only. The last tea service is at 2. Two day advance reservations are required and there is a one week cancellation policy. Groups of 2-50 are welcome.

Proprietors
Autograph_____Date_____

Country Cottage of Jacksonville

230 East C Street
Jacksonville, Oregon 97530
541-899-2900
Siege41@gmail.com

From I-5, take the Medford exit and follow Hwy 238 (Jacksonville Hwy) into Jacksonville. Watch for the white picket fence and arched gateway across from the Children's Historic Museum.

The Country Cottage Café, which is owned by Chris & Petra Georgiou, is a vintage house with a quiet view of Historic Jacksonville. It features garden murals indoors with pink and lavender wisteria vines hanging from the ceiling. Early Spring through Mid-Fall also offers outdoor seating on their scenic front porch.

The Queens Tea, priced at $20.00, is served with delightful sets of imported teapots and cups which are available for purchase. The tea starts with Perrier Water to make you comfortable, followed by a bowl of their home-made soup before a 3 tiered array of 6 varieties of finger sandwiches and quiche arrive. Endless pouring of tea brings a 3 tiered dessert tray filled with a variety of their homemade cookies, scones and desserts. Chris prepares all sandwiches & desserts personally and does the beautiful presentation. For tea, they choose the finest loose leaf tea's available and steam them to perfection.

Breakfast choices, priced from $5.95-$9.95, include crepes, omelets, bacon & Cheddar scramble, vegetarian quiche or oatmeal, served with a fresh fruit skewer, and from the bakery, a fresh blueberry muffin. Lunch features a "daily special" and a variety of great sandwiches- Reubens, turkey pepperoncini, French dip, hoagies or Philly's, as well as a vegetarian 3 cheese spinach & mushroom quiche or fresh daily baked chicken pot pie. They all come with a choice of green salad, home-made potato salad, or soup of the day plus fruit skewers for $10.95 to $12.95. The salad selection includes Chinese chicken, southwest and pepperoncini. Soups and salad are their specialty and all come with their home-made corn muffin or slices of artesian bread and fruit skewers for $5.95 to $10.95. For desserts the selection is extensive- raspberry lemon cheese cake, Nanaimo bars, brown sugar shortbread, pumpkin muffins, macaroons, their famous 4 layer chocolate midnight madness cake, and so much more. Business and party catering is also available.

Chris and Petra promise to make your day with them an enjoyable and memorable event. Take the time to stop by for one of their wonderful offerings!

MC/V/AMX/DEB/Checks
Wheelchair Accessible
4 Hour Free Street Parking

The Queens Tea is available Monday-Friday after 1:30, 24 hour reservations required. Breakfast is offered from 9-11 and lunch from11-3, 7 days a week.

Proprietors
Autograph_____Date_____

The Country Inn

4100 Country Farm Road
Eugene, Oregon 97408
541-343-7933
fax 541-343-7783

From I-5, take exit 195B to Beltline West. From Beltline, take the Coburg Road exit and proceed about 1½ miles. The Country Inn is on the left near the exit of Coburg Road and Game Farm Road.

This was one of those wonderful, accidental finds! While driving home from afternoon tea in Eugene, my friend Sue and I decided to take the old "country route" through Coburg. Along the way we passed this charming inn, and curiosity got the best of us. I turned around and we went back to investigate. The staff was welcoming and gave us the "cook's tour" of this former private residence.

We started our tour outside where we wandered around the beautiful garden. It featured a large gazebo which was surrounded by roses and other colorful flowers. Set to the sides of the garden were smaller gazebos and ponds with trickling waterfalls. The lawns were manicured and the trees and bushes trimmed to perfection!

Everything about the interior was beautiful and elegant. The rooms were on different levels which broke them up into intimate spaces. Toward the back of the house, a reception room features a beautiful old carved bar which practically takes up one complete wall. This room, the garden and other areas of the Inn are perfect locations for any event or special occasion.

Before leaving, I of course mentioned afternoon tea. As luck would have it, that is one of their offerings. Private teas can be arranged for small or large groups by special arrangement. If you are interested in spending the afternoon in this lovely setting, give Lisa a call.

MC/V/AE/DEB/Checks
Wheelchair Accessible
Lot Parking

Tea is by reservation only and there is a 72-hour cancellation policy. Teas are only offered in December.

Proprietors
Autograph_____Date___ _____

Cup of Blessings

Tea Cottage & Gifting Place
101 W. Second Street
Wallowa, Oregon 97885
541-886-4832
cupofblessings@localnet.com

The tea room is located one block off of Hwy 82. Turn left on Alder Street and go 1 block to the large parking area. There is a sign with a lady pouring tea that says Cup of Blessing and Gifting Place.

Scott and Judi Taylor opened their tea room in 2003 and molded it after Anne of Green Gables. The buildings were built to look like 1800 cottages– simple with a strong garden theme. Scott and Judy describe their tea room as a "tea garden" with ponds and paths, and many places to take tea. There is a private dining room for groups up to 6 and a Tea Pavilion that seats 40. Large groups are welcome and dessert buffets are one of their specialties. The hosts ask that you relax, enjoy each others company and find your meal worth waiting for!

Tea sets in the Tea Cup Cottage start with Anne's Full Tea for 2-6 persons for $36.50 pp. Allow 3 hours for this 5-course tea which includes-fruit cup, meat/cheese, assorted sandwiches, scones and dessert. Marilla's Tea offers a selection of tea sandwiches, scones and petite desserts for $26.50 and Matthew's Tea, priced at $22.50, has savory tea sandwiches, scones and a single serving dessert. The above teas include bottomless pots of tea and Cup of Blessings Devon cream and seasonal jams. Gratuity not included. Weather permitting, one may take one of the following teas in the Inspiration Garden and Tea Pavilion - Cream Tea for $7.50 or the Chocolate Dessert tea for a minimum of 6 guests for $16.95. Low Tea is offered for $16.50, and it includes assorted tea sandwiches, scones with Devon cream and jam, dessert and tea. Lunch is served by special request and is made to order on an individual basis.

The Taylor's have a gift shop where they sell their signature Heritage Teas and other tea time gifts. Judi does special tea programs upon request.

MC/V/AE/DEB/DIS/ Checks
Wheelchair Accessible
Lot and Free on-Street Parking

The shop is open Thursday-Friday-Saturday from 11-5. Tea time is by reservation only. The last tea service is 4 p.m. Reservations need to be made at least 48 hours in advance and there is a 48 hour cancellation policy. Some outside catering is available.

Proprietors
Autograph_____Date_____

Daughters of the British Empire

Tea, Bake Sale & Bazaar

Christ Episcopal Church
1060 Chandler Road
Lake Oswego, Oregon 97034

*From the South; take I-5 to exit 290 (Durham/Lake Oswego). Turn right on
Lower Boones Ferry Road, right on Country Club Road, then right on Chandler
(at 10th Street). From the North; take I-5 to Durham/Lake Oswego exit. Turn left
on Lower Boones Ferry Road, right on Country Club Road, and right on
Chandler (at 10th).*

The Daughters of the British Empire in Oregon is a non-profit, non-political, non-sectarian voluntary American Society of women of British or British Commonwealth ancestry. They support the British Home for retired men and women who are residents and/or citizens of the United States. They also raise funds for local charities such as the Oregon Food Bank. By attending this tea, you are helping this group of generous ladies contribute to the good of their community.

Presented annually since 1975, this special event tea is held in a church hall that is transformed into a tastefully decorated tea room, dressed in a beautiful Christmas Theme. Guests are seated at tables covered in linen cloths and the tea foods are served on heirloom bone china. Servers bring your tea and make sure that the cup is never empty! The tea plate offers tea sandwiches, savories and sweets, and the cost is $12 for adults and $6 for children under 12. While enjoying your tea, be mindful that you are under the watchful eye of the queen herself!

Before taking tea, or before heading for home, you will have the opportunity to make some special purchases at the bazaar and bake sale, which is set up in an adjoining room. Better yet, take advantage of both opportunities! You will find traditional British baked goods, Christmas crackers, Christmas Pudding and other British specialties. Some examples of hand crafted items are tea cozies, soaps, scarves, jewelry, ornaments and sachets.

I hope you will become one of the many who make this tea a Christmas tradition!

Cash/Checks
Wheelchair Accessible
Lot Parking

*This tea is offered once a year on the 3rd or 4th Saturday in November. Please refer to
the website, www.dbeoregon.org, for current information.*

Proprietors
Autograph_____Date_____

Historic Deepwood Estate

1116 Mission Street S.E.
Salem, Oregon 97302
503-363-1825
vist@historicdeepwoodestate.org
www.historicdeepwoodestate.org

From I-5, take exit 253 (Mission Street). Go west on Mission. Turn left on 12th.
The house is on the corner of Mission and 12th. The parking lot is on the corner
of 12th and Lee.

Deepwood Estate, which is owned by the city of Salem, is a beautifully restored 1894 Queen Ann style home and museum. Tea is served in the oak paneled dining room which also boasts beautiful stained glass windows and richly appointed carpet and fabrics ... the ambience of Victorian times.

Teas are presented each month and many of them are themed teas. The Dessert Tea is offered for $10 while the three course tea is available for $25. The cost of the teas includes a tour of the home and a stroll through the ever-changing five and a half acres of English Gardens. Some of the teas are prepared especially for children.

Deepwood is considered one of the finest examples of a Queen Anne home west of the Mississippi and here you will experience tea as it was. Past attendees have said, "It was the best I have ever experienced - I feel thoroughly pampered!"

You will have an opportunity to choose from a selection of unique gifts which are set out and available for purchase. Many of the items are tea related while others will tempt those who are swept away by all things vintage.

Have a wonderful tea and know that your presence contributes to the preservation of this lovely "lady."

MC/V/Checks
No Wheelchair Access
Lot Parking

Teas are by reservation only, and refunds may be requested up to 5 days in advance of the event. Call Deepwood Estate for dates and times of public teas. Private teas can be arranged for a minimum of 16 guests.

Proprietors
Autograph_____Date_____

38

The Doll House Tea Room

3223 S.E. Risley Avenue
Milwaukie, Oregon 97267
503-653-6809
info@dolhousetearoom.com
www.dollhousetearoom.com

Take I-205 to the Oregon City exit, turn right on 99E and go about 4 miles toward Milwaukie. Watch for GI Joe's. Turn left at the next street (Risley Avenue). The tea room is the first driveway on the right.

Opened in 2000 by Jeanine Nordling, The Doll House Tea Room truly fits its name. Every room is decorated with whimsical painted chairs, tea pots with fresh flowers on the tables, and beautiful dolls. Pretty pastel tablecloths, attractive wall borders and soft curtains with floral touches complete the look.

Jeanine has been offering "Fabulous Dress-up Tea Parties" for little girls for 7½ years. The Fantasy Closet is complete with 150+ gowns and accessories for girls of all ages, with sizes from 2T to 20 women.

This is a little girl's fantasy come true and a special experience to cherish always. At the end of a party, the little girls (aged 4 to 14) either want to live here or work here! Parties include: printed, personalized invitations, gowns and accessories, a trip to the salon for hair, nails and makeup and a fashion show with keepsake photo. A complete lunch is served on child-sized china on tables with lots of fresh flowers, party favors, a birthday cake and a special keepsake for the guest of honor. There are thank you notes and lots of personalizing to make the birthday girl feel like a queen for the day. There is no prep, clean up, shopping or creativity for mom to worry about. Just come and watch the party while our staff waits on the children and you enjoy relaxing with a cup of tea or coffee and cookies. Prices and additional information are available on the website, www.dollhousetearoom.com.

MC/V/DEB/Checks
Not Wheelchair Accessible
Lot and Street Parking

Open Wednesday, Thursday and Friday for adult teas. Tea time is 11-3:30 with the last tea service at 2:30. Open Saturdays for dress-up parties. Reservations are recommended 24-hours in advance. Groups of 12 or more will be charged a non-refundable deposit if cancelled in less that 48-hours.

Proprietors
Autograph_____Date_____

Ermatinger House

619 - 6th Street
Oregon City, Oregon 97045
503-650-1851
harding63@att.net

From Hwy 99 in Oregon City, take 10th Street up Singer Hill (the street to the upper level of town). At the top, 10th becomes 7th Street. Turn right and go to 6th Street. Take a left and go to 619-6th. It is on the corner of 6th and John Adams.

Francis Ermatinger came to Oregon in 1835 as an employee of the Hudson's Bay Company. He worked his way up through the ranks under Dr. John McLoughlin, the father of Oregon, and was placed in charge of the Company store in Oregon City in 1844. He was later elected treasurer of Oregon's Provisional Government. His house, which he built in 1845, was the first frame house built in Oregon and only the third in the entire Oregon County. Due to the development around Willamette Falls, in 1910 the house was moved to the upper level of town. In 1986, the Ermatinger House was moved to its present location at 6th and John Adams.

The Ermatinger House welcomes groups for a Living History Tea and tour by reservation, and they are conducted by Marge Harding. Marge takes guests back to the period of the Oregon Trail and early Oregon history, and she speaks in first person while sharing the "news of the day." Comments and questions by guests are pertinent to "today." As Marge says, "you are eating in 1865."

The afternoon tea, which is enjoyed during the presentation, includes scones with lemon curd and Devon cream, fruit, sandwiches, shortbread and tea for $16. A Full Tea, which adds Quiche to the afternoon tea, is offered for $19. These special teas are a fun learning experience with good food....a perfect combination!

Cash/Checks
Not Wheelchair Accessible
Street Parking

Living History Teas are by special arrangement only. Private tours may be arranged. Admission is $4 for adults and $3 for seniors and students.

Proprietors
Autograph_____Date_____

Eve's Garden Café & Tea Room

15090 Highway 238
Applegate, Oregon 97530
541-846-9019
evesgardencafe@gmail.com
www.edengatefarm.com

From I-5, take exit 58 at Grants Pass and proceed to intersection for Williams Hwy/Hwy 238. Take that highway toward Murphy and continue to the town of Applegate. From I-5 in Medford, take exit 30 and head west on Hwy 238 through the town of Jacksonville. Continue another 15 miles to the town of Applegate.

Eve's Garden Café, which is owned by Cathy and Bill, opened in 2002 at Eden's Gate Farms in historic Applegate. The quaint tea room is located in a 1890s cottage and boasts a whimsical décor complete with painted clouds on the ceiling and ivy on the floor. The windows are decorated with antique hankie valances, and the tables are covered with antique cloths. Outside seating is offered in the summer in their beautiful rose and flower gardens. What better setting for dress-up tea parties featuring Victorian hats, vintage attire, gloves and boas? Cathy and Bill call their parties, "a great escape for a few hours of fun."

"Tea Time" is offered all day for $14 and it includes a scone with Devon Cream and lemon curd, three tea sandwiches, two desserts and a pot of tea. Reservations are not required.

High Tea, which is by reservation only, would be the perfect event for an anniversary, shower, retirement, business luncheon, or any other special occasion. At a cost of $14.95 for children and $21.95 for adults, the tea offers scones with Devonshire cream and lemon curd, soup or salad, finger sandwiches and quiche, an assortment of desserts and a selection of teas to choose from for your bottomless pot of tea.

Breakfast items such as French toast made with hazelnut bread or a croissant sandwich are also offered. Lunch specialties include quiche, salads, sandwiches and soups. You might be tempted to try Eatin' from the Garden, a double-decker vegetarian sandwich or Gobble Till You Wobble, the cook's favorite turkey sandwich.

Catering is available for groups up to 25 during the winter and for up to 125 in the summer. The tea room shares space with a gift shop so allow yourself time to browse in this "little bit of heaven."

MC/V/DEB/Cash, Wheelchair Accessible, Lot Parking

Summer hours: Wednesday through Friday 10-3 and Saturday and Sunday 9-3. Winter hours are Wednesday through Sunday 10-3. High tea is by reservation only. Your credit card will be charged if you fail to show at the appointed time. A gratuity is added for groups of 5 or more.

Proprietors
Autograph_____Date_____

Gardner House Café

& Bed & Breakfast

633 N. 3rd Street
Stayton, Oregon 97383
503-769-5478
www.gardnerhousebnb.com

From I-5, go east 13 miles to the Stayton/Sublimity exit. Turn right toward Stayton. That is Cascade Hwy and it turns into 1st. Street. Turn left on Washington (3rd light), go 2 blocks and turn right. Proceed 1 block and look for the gazebo and 3-tiered fountain on your right.

James and Loni Loftus opened their business in the summer of 2008 in a lovely old Victorian, which happens to be the oldest home in Stayton. The ground floor offers 2 rooms for your dining pleasure and a well stocked bakery case to tempt you. The rooms feature yellow walls and antique tables topped with pink cloths and white linen napkins. Old and interesting pictures abound on the walls and beckon you to "visit" them.

There are 4 tea set choices to choose from, starting with the Mini Tea which offers a fresh fruit cup and choice of scone or muffin for $5.95 or the Dessert Tea for $7.95. The Light Tea includes a fresh fruit cup, savory tart, assorted sandwiches and dessert for $12.95. Finally, the High Tea offers fresh fruit cup, choice of scone, savory tart, assorted sandwiches and dessert for $18. The last two teas require reservations. All include choice of tea.

This is a café so other offerings are available - breakfast items, lunch specialties and numerous pastries, cookies and desserts. There is also an extensive selection of beverages including specialty coffees and Italian sodas. The tea menu has many interesting choices, from traditional black blends to my favorite - rooibos. Advance notice required for special dietary needs.

If you happen to be here on a warm day, you can choose to take your meal on the lawn under the Gazebo. This is interesting, because sitting outside gives you a chance to take in the architecture of this wonderful painted lady. There is also a conference room available for meetings or small gatherings.

MC/Visa/Debit
Handicapped Accessible
Street Parking,

They are open Monday-Saturday from 6:30 a.m. to 6 p.m. High tea is offered daily from 11 to 3. Reservations are recommended.

Proprietors
Autograph_____Date_____

Gates House Tea Room

525-10th Avenue S.W.
Albany, Oregon 97321
541-926-1511
gateshouse@hotmail.com

From Pacific in Albany take Washington Street then take a right on 10th Street. From Corvallis, take Hwy.20, go right on 9th Street, left on Washington and left on 10th. The house is half way down the block on the right.

Shawn Nevin has been very fortunate to be able to follow her passion by opening her very own tea room in 2007. She offers tea in her charming home, which is located in the renowned Albany Historic District. Upon entering the Queen Anne home, one feels that they have indeed found the calm that tea time offers. There are two rooms dedicated to tea - the Pansy Tea Room and The Cobalt Blue Room. Both are true to their names and are filled with lovely and interesting décor. .For larger groups, Shawn sets an additional table next to the cobalt room. This table carries a pink depression glass theme.

The home is welcoming and guests are invited to take a peek at the antique and collectable filled rooms on the main floor. Your time with Shawn will be a pleasurable experience with a very friendly and warm lady. She delights in making your tea time experience memorable!

The tea menu is pre-arranged by you and is offered at a cost of $12. There is a selection of 4 salads, 4 sandwiches and 6 desserts to choose from. You are able to pick one side salad, two sandwiches and two desserts, all of which are very tasty. You also pre-select 2 teas.

After taking tea, it is a short jaunt to the downtown district where you can find numerous antique and collectable shops to visit before heading home.

Cash/Checks
Not wheelchair accessible
Free Street Parking

Teas are by reservation only, at least 2 days in advance. The tea room can accommodate from 2 to 14 people. Close on Sunday. The last teatime is 3. Theme teas are offered.

Proprietors
Autograph_____Date_____

Gentle House

345 N. Monmouth Avenue
Monmouth, Oregon 97361
503-838-8673
gentlehouse@wou.edu
www.wou.edu/president/advancement/gentle/

From Hwy 99W, go west on Main Street (the four-way traffic light for Monmouth and Independence). Travel six blocks to a four-way stop and turn right onto North Monmouth Avenue. Travel through campus. Gentle House is on the right, just past the Oregon Military Academy and Gentle Avenue.

This beautiful historic home, situated on nearly 4 acres of landscaped gardens, was the home of Thomas Gentle and his family. Built in the early 1880s, the farmhouse was purchased by Thomas in 1914. He was the head of Campus Elementary Training at Oregon Normal School, which is now Western Oregon University. The home remained in the family until daughter Catharine donated it to the WOU Foundation in 1981. She asked that it be used by the college and community for "genteel entertaining." What better way to use the home than for afternoon tea.

In 2004, an energetic committee started planning Tea Party Luncheons as fundraisers for Gentle House. They planned menus, sewed tea cozies and napkins, and started a collection of tea cups. Their efforts were well rewarded, as each tea has been well attended. A typical tea is a buffet, and it features a delicious selection of finger sandwiches, scones, fruit trays and a selection of petite desserts. Everything is presented on doily-lined tiered servers and pretty serving plates. The cost of a typical tea is between $14 and $20, which is an excellent value for a benefit tea.

The tables are set about the house, and are covered with soft-colored tablecloths that coordinate with the napkins and cozies. Fresh flower nosegays in teapots are set in the center of the table. For some of the teas, entertainment is provided by the WOU music department.

How satisfying it is to take tea in an historic home while helping support that home.

MC/V/Checks
Wheelchair Accessible
Lot Parking

Teas are offered on special occasions during the year. Please call for more information. They are by reservation only. There are three seating for tea - 11, 12:15 and 1:30.

Proprietors
Autograph_____Date_____

The Gordon House

Next door to the Oregon Garden

879 West Main Street
Silverton, Oregon 97381
503-874-6006 / 877-674-2733 ext. 6006
molly@thegordonhouse.org
www.thegordonhouse.org

The house is located on Main Street at the south end of Silverton and only 15 miles east of Salem on Silverton Road.

We have had the pleasure of visiting both The Gardens and the Gordon House in Silverton. Having grown up hearing about Frank Lloyd Wright, it was especially memorable to be able to visit the only house in Oregon that was designed by him. It is also his only building open to the public in the Northwest. How sad it would have been had the house been destroyed!

I met Molly, the site manager at a tea class we took together. Her interest in tea, and her desire to present teas which will benefit the Gordon House, are note-worthy.

Teas are presented at noon during specific holidays of the year and reservations need to be made from two months to two days in advance, as available. The setting is a home that features Frank Lloyd Wright's "economic design for middle-class American families." It provides the tea attendees a unique and artistic setting for tea and lunch. How special it is for us to be able to sit down and relax as a guest of the Gordon House!

The tea venue changes from tea to tea and some of the menus follow a particular theme. An example would be the Russian Tea, in honor of Wright's wife Olgivanne: Russian Caravan black tea, Georgia black tea, Honey Lemon Ginseng Herb tea, cream scones with fig jam and lime curd, salmon quiche with medium Cheddar cheese, and finger sandwiches of herbed cream cheese with cucumber. A seasonal squash soup and Anastasia cake complete the meal, which costs $35 ($30 members). A tour of the house is presented after lunch. Sounds wonderful!

The best part about taking tea at the Gordon House is that the proceeds continue the restoration and preservation of this very special house.

MC/V Checks
Wheelchair Accessible
Free Parking

Tea is by reservation only and is offered in November, December and February on Saturdays at noon. Total seating capacity is 25-40 people and groups are welcome.

Proprietors
Autograph_____Date_____

The Heathman Restaurant

1001 S.W. Broadway at Salmon
Portland, Oregon 97205
503-790-7752
www.heathmanrestaurantandbar.com

The restaurant is located in the Heathman Hotel at the corner of Broadway and Salmon in downtown Portland.

 The Heathman Restaurant calls its Afternoon Tea "a long standing and cherished tradition in Portland." This stately Old World hotel offers tea in the elegant lobby amid sparkling chandeliers, wood paneling and eucalyptus. A working fireplace adds to the charm of this historic tea room.

 The afternoon tea, priced at $32 per person, includes smoked salmon profiteroles, chicken salad panini, goat cheese crostini, classic cucumber sandwich, deviled egg, Heathman scone, Lanai banana bread, Parisian opera cake, Haupia (Hawaiian style coconut cake), lemon bar, devil's food chocolate tea cupcake, house-made marshmallows and a pot of tea. The Peter Rabbit Tea for "little sippers" consists of a peanut butter and jelly sandwich, cheese blocks, gold fish, carrot sticks with ranch dip, fresh fruit, "ants on a log", snickerdoodle, coconut cake, banana bread, chocolate cupcake and hot chocolate for $14. Sparkling and Sweets by the glass are also available. The house tea is Fonte Coffee and Tea Co. out of Seattle, Washington, and there is a generous selection of regular and decaffeinated teas. Coffee is available upon request, as is a full lunch menu.

MC/V/DIS/CB/AE and Checks Accepted
The Lobby is Wheelchair Accessible
Metered Street Parking

Their Holiday Tea is offered from the day after Thanksgiving to New Years weekend at 11, 1, and 3. Afternoon tea is offered Monday through Friday at 2 and Saturday and Sunday at 12 and 2. Reservations are required, preferably 48 hours in advance.

Proprietors
Autograph_____Date_____

Hoffman House

523 E. Main Street
Molalla, Oregon 97038
503-829-2640
hoffmanhouse@molalla.net
www.hoffmanhouserestaurant.net

From I-5, take the Woodburn exit and head east (Hwy 214). Continue for 20 minutes to Molalla, where the road changes to Hwy 211 Main Street. They are in the historic downtown area on the corner of Main and Fenton, in the two story house with blue trim and the large front yard.

Originally built by the Robbins family in 1888, this Folk Victorian home housed the first library in Molalla from 1900 to 1906. Dennis and Debbie Hoffman took on the task of restoring this historic building and transformed it into the Hoffman House Restaurant, which they opened in 2003.

Debbie offers a number of special teas. The High Tea, which is priced at $18, includes tea, cantaloupe bisque or fruit in season, scone with cream and lemon curd, tea sandwiches and savories, and assorted sweets. It is prepared for a minimum of 10 guests and requires 2 weeks advance reservation. Two different teas of your choice are served throughout the party. Please allow 1 1/2 to 2 hours for your tea party.

The Children's Craf-tea is $16 per person and there is an 8 person minimum. Tea is served on fine china and there is a plate of fruit and sandwiches and other delights that children love. "Dirt cake" is served in a flower pot with gummy worms and a flower. After the cake is finished, the children enjoy a craft time of decorating their flower pot which they take home with them. The birthday girl is treated to a tiara and a cape to make her feel special.

Other teas are the Afternoon Tea for $10 which includes tea, scone, 2 tea sandwiches and 2 sweets, the Sweet Tea for $8 and the Cream Tea for $6.

The dinner menu includes such items as Shrimp for $12.95, Country Fried Steak for $8.95 and Catfish for $10.95. They feature Prime Rib every Friday night starting at 5 while supplies last. Appetizers are available, and the entreés include chefs' choice of vegetable and potato and your choice of soup or salad.

V/MC/Checks
Wheelchair Accessible
Street Parking

They are open Monday-Thursday 11-8 and Friday-Saturday 11-9. Tea parties are by special reservations.

Proprietors
Autograph_____Date_____

Kashin Tei Tea House

611 S.W. Kingston Avenue
Portland, Oregon 97201
503-223-9233
ldieken@japanesegarden.com
www.japanesegarden.com

The Tea House is located west of the Rose Gardens and tennis courts in Washington Park. Call the Japanese Garden Society at 503-223-4070 for specific directions.

This authentic 4½ mat tea room from Japan, whose name translates to Flower Heart Hut, is owned and operated by the Japanese Garden Society of Oregon. The tea presentation may be viewed by the public May through September, on the 3rd Saturday of the month from 1 to 2. This is during the Japanese Garden operating hours.

Private party experiences for 5-10 guests are available for a fee of $100 and up. Guests will be served a Japanese tea sweet and bowl of Matcha, which is a powdered green tea.

To arrange a private experience of Chanoya (tea of water) or Chado (path of tea), call the Japanese Tea Society and they will provide the names and phone numbers of certified teachers.

The Japanese Garden has a gift shop for your enjoyment.

Not Wheelchair Accessible
Lot Parking and On Street Parking.

Call the Japanese Garden Society for specific information.

Proprietors
Autograph_____Date_____

La Tea Da Tea Room

904 Main Avenue
Tillamook, Oregon 97140
503-842-5447
lateadatearoom@embarqmail.com
www.lateada-tearoom.com

The tea room is located at the corner of Main and 9th streets. This is Hwy 101, and is a one-way street going south.

   La Tea Da is gaining a reputation as "the place to go" for tea. The beautiful tea room, opened in 2001 by Terry and Suzanne, says welcome, come in and relax. Its lavender and pale yellow walls, lovely floral arrangements, eclectic collection of antique furnishings, and lace window coverings are just the perfect touches. If seating is not available right away, you can take advantage of the wait by looking through the wonderful gift shop. It features hand-painted teapots and teacups, silver serving pieces, English bone china and imported jams, jellies and teas - the essential ingredients for taking tea at home. Unique picture frames, tassels, swags, Tiffany-style lamps, candles and bath products are also available for purchase. If you wish, complimentary gift wrapping is included.
   Once seated in the tea room, sit back and take in the surroundings while you make your choice from the numerous tea sets. One may choose the Queen Mum's tea, which offers something sweet, or the Cuppa Tea, with its three scones. The Villagers Tea consists of sorbet and soup with scones or tea sandwiches and the Governors Tea, preferred by gentlemen, consists of sorbet, a selection of sandwiches and savories, scones and a little sweet. The tea that receives raves is the La Tea Da High Tea! This 4-course tea starts with sorbet, followed by sandwiches and savories. Then, one sweet and one Tillamook cheese scone are served, followed by a selection of dainty and ever-so-tasty desserts. All of the teas include a pot of tea and the scones are served with clotted cream and lemon curd. For the children, there is a Scamp's tea with bite-sized sandwiches and sweets, sorbet and a whimsical tot's pot of tea for $6.95. There is something for everyone and every morsel is delicious! Special event teas are offered.

MC/V/AE/DIS/Checks
Wheelchair Accessible
Free Street Parking

Summer hours are Monday-Saturday, 10:30-5:30 and winter hours are Tuesday-Saturday 10:30-5:30. Tea is served from 11 to 4. Reservations are recommended, groups are welcome, and a party room is available for a small fee.

Proprietors
Autograph_____Date_____

Lady Di's British Store

& Tea Room

430 Second Street
Lake Oswego, Oregon 97034
503-635-7298
800-357-7839

From I-205 take exit 8 to West Linn and follow HWY 43 to Lake Oswego. Turn left at A Avenue and right on Second Street. From 1-5 take 1st exit after the Markham Bridge (Hwy 43 /Lake Oswego). Follow signs to Lake Oswego. Turn right at A Avenue and right on 2nd Street.

Lady Di, with its convenient location, has been a mainstay in Lake Oswego for a number of years. The store opened in 1986, and Moya added the tea room in 2000. The shelves in the grocery area are stocked with a large selection of British groceries and teas. There are frozen and refrigerated items available for purchase as well. An extensive catalog serves those who can't make it into the shop, but who long for goods from their homeland.

Collectibles, such as teapots, cards, miniatures, pictures and other English items are set about the store to tempt you.

Tucked away in a corner, enclosed by a friendly fence, is the vine-clad tea room where one can enjoy a cup of tea and quiet conversation. Moya offers a varied menu from which one can select a tasty morsel to enjoy with tea. You may choose a sandwich platter with crisps and fruit for $9.95 or the Lady Di Tea which includes tea sandwiches, warm savories, scone with Devon cream and strawberry preserves, mini desserts, shortbread and a pot of tea for one priced at $14.95. If you prefer to have just a scone, there is a Devon Cream Tea for $7.50 which includes a pot of tea for one. A special holiday tea is offered at Christmas time. The traditional English Ploughman's Lunch is available for $9.95 and soup and sandwiches can be purchased a la carte.

Special dietary needs can be accommodated with advance request.

MC/V/AE/DEB/Checks
Wheelchair accessible
Free Street Parking

Store hours Monday through Saturday 10-5. Teatime is 11-3:30. There is seating for 18 people in the Garden area and the small English Parlor seats 6. Reservations are required a few days in advance for Saturday tea and for groups.

Proprietors
Autograph_____Date_____

Lavender Tea House

& Gift Shop

16227 S.W. 1st Avenue
Sherwood, Oregon 97140
503-625-4479
LavenderTeaHouse@yahoo.com
www.lavenderteahouse.com

From 99W, turn south onto North Sherwood Boulevard (light). Follow for almost a mile (0.8), turn right onto 1st Street. They are 2 1/2 blocks down on the right.

The location of Lavender Tea House, an 1892 Queen Anne Victorian cottage, couldn't be more suitable ... across from a park with a huge aging tree, near the end of the street in a quaint neighborhood. The new owner, Jamie Yang, has spent a great deal of time remodeling the tea room which now features a "special" bakery and a Tea Bar. Jamie has also updated the menu.

The LTH High Tea is a full tea experience. It begins with flutes of sparkling cider followed by a delicious bowl of soup. Traditional tiered servers present scones, tea sandwiches, savories, fruit and mini pastries. The LTH tea is $25 and must be pre-ordered prior to arrival. The new 2½ hr. Silver Tea Service is an event in itself. Priced at $90 for 2 people, "this tea is reserved only for those who truly appreciate the art of tea service and table top." The menu includes sparkling cider, tea & coffee, soup, salad, sorbet, a beautiful tier full of LTH specialties-scones, tea sandwiches, savories, fruit, and mini pastries. There is a 2 person minimum and 4 person maximum and this tea must be pre-arranged, pre-paid and ordered prior to arrival.

For the smaller appetites, there are a number of other offerings on the luncheon menu. Queen Mum has 4 tea sandwiches, scone with jam & clotted cream and fresh fruit for $10.75, with choice of beverage extra. The Garden has 4 tea sandwiches, seasonal fruit and dessert for $9.75, with beverage choice extra. A Cream Tea is offered for $8.50 and a Dessert Tea is $9. There is a Child's Tea for $9 as well as other lighter fare items. The gift shop offers that perfect gift or memento to commemorate your visit ... tea pots, books, linens and much more. Allow yourself time to look around and to try a new tea at the tea bar.

MC/V/DEB/Checks
Wheelchair Accessible
Free Street Parking

The bakery is open from 7 a.m. to 7 p.m. seven days a week. Tea is served Tuesday through Saturday at 9, 11:15 and 1:30 and on Sunday at 9 and 11:15.

Proprietors
Autograph_____Date_____

Leach Botanical Garden

6704 S.E. 122nd Avenue
Portland, Oregon. 97236
503-823-9503-executive assistant
www.leachgarden.org

From I-205, turn east onto Foster Road. Go to 122nd and turn right. You will go down a hill and across a short bridge to the parking lot. The walk up to the house is across from the parking lot.

Though tea is only offered once a year, it is an excellent one and worth putting on your calendar well in advance. On one weekend in July, Leach Garden offers a fundraising tea for $25 per person. Tea is served in three courses with a first course of scones with jam, Devonshire jam and butter patties. The second course, which offers 4 selections, might consist of such delectables as a fruit cup, asparagus rolls, dilly cucumber rounds, Persian chicken packets, or tomato with basil and mozzarella cheese. For the finale, which includes 4 items, perhaps you will enjoy poppy seed cake, lemon curd tart, raspberry shortbread or chocolate truffle. What ever the menu, and it changes each year, you will be pleased with the taste and presentation. You will also be entertained and treated royally by the wonderful servers who are the spouses of members.

Tea is served outdoors on a brick terrace adjacent to the house. Each table is set with a different color theme that includes china, flowers and table cloths. China is varied patterns but matching colors. Lovely floral center-pieces grace the tables and each guest's plate is decorated with edible flowers and herbs.

Large groups can be accommodated but must be willing to sit at separate assigned tables, as their largest table is for 10. They can place the party's tables in close proximity to each other. Well, wouldn't this be the perfect opportunity to meet new tea friends?

There is a gift shop, so allow yourself a little extra time to look around after you have toured the gardens and enjoyed this wonderful tea. The gardens are open year round so if you can't make it for tea, stop by for a tour any time when they are open.

MC/V/DEB/Checks
Wheelchair Accessible
Free Lot Parking

The gardens are open Tuesday through Saturday 9-4 and Sunday 1-4. Tea is offered one Saturday in July only, by reservation only. The seatings are noon and 2:30. Call early in May for the date and to make reservations.

Proprietors
Autograph_____Date_____

Lisa's Tea Room

1520 Main Street
Philomath, Oregon 97370
541-929-7700

From I-5, take Hwy 34/20 toward Corvallis. Stay on 34 and about 5 miles west of Corvallis, you will enter Philomath on a one-way going west. You will see the tea room on the left but you have to pass it and take the next left (Chevron station). Take another left after McDonalds and stay on that one way as it curves. The tea room is on your immediate right after the curve. Watch for the driveway. They are across from the Wells Fargo bank.

Lisa moved from her downtown Corvallis location to a charming cottage on the main street in Philomath in 2006. The location has changed but not the wonderful food and service. As you enter you find a casual country themed dining area and gift area to your left. On the right, a beautiful formal dining table, covered in a floor length white table cloth, is placed in front of the picture window. A candelabra is centered over the table and beautiful china and crystal grace the table. Soft chairs, covered completely in white material, finish the theme. More gifts are displayed on numerous shelves in the area. As you venture to the back rooms you enter a formal English style dining room which features deep colors and floral designs. Finally, the Children's room has an Alice in Wonderland theme where white tables and chairs invite you to visit. Racks about the room are laden with stuffed animals, collectable dolls and many items to tempt young customers or the child in you.

Afternoon tea sets, as well as casual teas, are plated or served on tiered servers and range in price from $5.50 to $15.25. They offer tasty scones, fresh sandwiches, warm savories, seasonal fruit and moist desserts. There is also a Children's Tea for the young tea enthusiast.

For those who prefer lunch, Lisa offers sandwiches, salads and quiche for $8.50 to $9.75. All lunches include a bowl of soup. The house tea is Harney and Sons, but for the coffee lover, that is available as well. A revolving glass display case offers many of Lisa's signature desserts to complete your meal.

This is a great destination tea room and also a place to take a break on the way to the coast.

MC/V/DEB/DIS/Checks
Wheelchair Accessible
Lot Parking

The tea room is open Thursday through Saturday from 11 to 3. Reservations are suggested and cancellations are accepted up to the day before the scheduled visit. Groups may reserve any day with a minimum. Call for specifics. Special teas are offered with the seasons and on Valentines Day.

Proprietors
Autograph_____Date_____

Lovejoys Tea Room

& Restaurant
195 Nopal Street
Florence, Oregon 97439
541-902-0502
www.lovejoysrestaurant.com

Going north on Hwy 101, cross the Florence Bridge. Before coming to the first stop light, turn right on Nopal Street. Continue on Nopal to the corner of 1st Street. Going south, just before the Florence Bridge, turn left on Nopal.

Located in Old Town Florence, and established in 2003 by Judith and Liam Kingsmill, this charming tea room has all of the ambience one would expect in a traditional British tea room.

Featuring an elevated dining area, the room is rich in color with its deep red curtains on the six large corner windows and coordinated textured carpet. The walls are a golden yellow, and large gold-hued roses serve as curtain tie-backs. Antique furnishings, framed art and tables covered in floral cloths complete the elegant look.

The tea choices begin with a Cream Tea for $6.95 and a Light Tea of one sandwich, scones and a petite dessert for $8.95. High Tea, which is $12.95 for 1 and $21 for 2, includes two tea sandwiches, two salads, scones, and a petite dessert. The final presentation is the Royal Tea which offers a sandwich selection, 2 salads, savory, petit four and scone priced at 2 for $27. All teas include your choice of Taylors of Harrogate tea, and double Devon cream and lemon curd or preserves for your scones.

The lunch menu includes hot items, salads, soups and sandwiches. Salmon Bisque is available every day and there is a lunch special that changes weekly. Check the website for specials. Coffee, beer, wine and espresso are also available. Dietary needs can be accommodated with advance arrangements.

A gift area carries imported tea items such as tea pots and cozies. Bulk teas - Taylors of Harrogate, P.G. Tips and Typhoo, as well as many English grocery items, are also available for purchase.

MC/V/Checks/Cash
Wheelchair Accessible
Street and Lot Parking

Summer hours are 11-4 Tuesday through Saturday and winter hours are 11-3 Tuesday through Saturday. Any time is teatime. Reservations are suggested 48-hours in advance. Groups up to 30 people are welcome.

Proprietors
Autograph_____Date_____

Mon Ami

490 Highway 101
Florence, Oregon 97439
541-997-9234
cindywobbe@msn.com

*From Hwy 126 East, turn left onto Hwy 101. The tea room is located next to the
Purple Pelican Antique Mall, at the corner of Hwy 101 and Rhododendron.*

Mon Ami is among the many tea rooms making an appearance on the Oregon coast.
A really adventurous soul could spend a couple of days just driving from one to another
while seeing the beautiful sights and listening to the wonderful sounds of the ocean!

The tea room tables are located amid a wonderful collection of antiques and
collectibles, all of which will tempt you while you are waiting for tea to be served. Seems
I never stay seated very long, as I find myself browsing between courses. Not to worry,
Cindy never rushes you!

The High Tea, which is served in three courses, includes assorted tea sandwiches and
canapés, Mon Ami's signature Waldorf salad, freshly baked scones with citrus curd,
classic shortbread, delicate desserts and a pot of tea for $13.95. If you are looking for a
little lighter fare, there is a Petite Luncheonette which includes a delicious salad, two tea
sandwiches (may include quiche if available), fresh scones and shortbread with citrus
curd and clotted cream and a petite dessert. Dietary needs may be accommodated with
advance notice and they are "Adkins friendly!" The house tea is Taylors of Harrogate and
they offer that, as well as other labels, for sale. Holiday teas are presented and they would
be "happy to do special theme teas" for your special occasion.

This is a great area of town to do some browsing, so allow yourself plenty of time to
check out Mon Ami as well as the other stores around it.

If a stay in the area is in your plans, Cindy now operates a beautifully decorated guest
cottage overlooking the ocean. It is 20 miles north of Florence near Yachats and is called
Sea Mist Guest Cottage. Many of their out-of-town customers stay there and then go to
Mon Ami for tea.

MC/V/DIS/Checks
Wheelchair accessible but please let them know you are coming.
Free Street and Lot Parking

*Open Monday through Friday 9:30-5 and on Saturday 9:30-5. They are closed on
Sunday. All teas are by reservation only.*

Proprietors
Autograph_____Date_____

Moyer House Benefit Tea

East Blakely Avenue
Brownsville, Oregon 97327
541-401-0500
karenengel@comcast.net

The tea is held at the former Brownsville Elementary School, which is located on East Blakely Avenue in Brownsville.

The elegant Moyer House was built by John and Elizabeth Moyer in 1881. The house was inspired by Italianate Villa-style, popular at the time, but was an original design. The exterior is generously decorated with carved finials, corner boards, frieze boards and eave brackets.

The Moyers were early Linn County settlers who were influential in the development of Brownsville. Elizabeth was the daughter of Hugh L. Brown, for whom Brownsville was named. She met John while he helped her father build the house. They were married in 1857 and first lived in a house outside of town. They later moved to town and John ran a successful planing mill as well as the woolen mill. John and Elizabeth lived in the house together until his death in 1900. Elizabeth continued to live there until her death in 1920. In 1963 the Linn County Historical Society acquired the house with a grant and private donations. The house now belongs to Linn County and is designated a museum, under the care of the Parks Department and a group of volunteers.

Karen Engel, a devoted volunteer, heads-up the committee which puts on this annual benefit tea. She first found a location, as the tea can't be held at Moyer House, and now enlists hostesses to take care of centerpieces, dishes, linens and favors, all of which follow a theme … most of them the holidays.

I had the pleasure of attending this tea where I enjoyed delicious scones, served with clotted cream and jam, 3 tea sandwiches, 2 cookies, 2 dessert bars, chocolates and unlimited tea. The menu changes with each tea and entertainment is provided. I can't think of a better way to honor a lovely old house than to attend a benefit tea in her honor and to visit Moyer House before or after tea in Brownsville.

Checks/Cash
Wheelchair Accessible
Lot Parking

The tea is held on the first Saturday in December. Seating is limited to 200 and is by advance ticket sales only. The cost is $25 and a portion of the cost is tax-deductible. Mail reservations to Karen Engel, 730 Washington Street S.E., Albany, Oregon, 97321. Please include a self-addressed stamped envelope.

Proprietors
Autograph_____Date_____

Mrs. B's Special Teas

55 West Grant
Lebanon, Oregon 97355
541-259-5100
tea@mrsbtea.com
www.mrsbtea.com

From I-5, go east on Hwy 34 (Exit 228 / Corvallis). Go straight until you get to a "T." Turn right then right again on 2nd Street. Proceed to second stop sign (Grant and turn right.) They are the second building on the right.

The Tudor-style building on Grant Street has housed Mrs. B's Special Teas since 2000, and it is a wonderful destination for afternoon tea. The owner, Barbara Brown, has dedicated the tea room to the memory of her very special mother, Gatha Viola, and her love of all things tea is evident in the food, ambience and service.

When you enter the shop, your eyes are drawn to the beautiful Victorian Tea Room in the corner with the large chandelier and the deep burgundy walls. The color scheme changes monthly to suit that month's holiday. Everything changes … tablecloths, glassware, teapots, candles, dishes and even the many collectibles which adorn the shelves that encircle the room above you.

The tiered servers, with the appropriate colored flowers, feature a special sandwich to match the theme. There are a number of teas to choose from: The Royal Tea of sandwiches and scone or desserts at $12, the Luncheon Tea with sandwiches, scone and assorted desserts for $14.50, and the four-course Victorian Tea for $18 and the five-course Queen's Tea at $21. The latter two feature five desserts! All include Devon Cream, preserves and all the tea you can drink. Gourmet coffee is also available.

I recommend that you plan to arrive early or stay late, because the gift area is very large and ever so interesting. You will find everything from cards, books and teapots to boas, hats and a "sea of red and purple!" Take your time checking - out because all the fun jewelry is near the cash register and you are bound to get distracted!

MC/V/Check
Wheelchair Accessible
Street Parking and Lot

The shop is open 9-5:30 Tuesday through Friday. Tea is offered with 24 hour advance reservation, from 11-2. Lunch is available every day and special dinners are presented on Friday nights. The maximum number of guests is 26. Theme and holiday teas are offered throughout the year.

Proprietors
Autograph_____Date_____

Newell House Museum

at Champoeg State Park

8089 Champoeg Road N.E.
Saint Paul, Oregon 97137
503-678-5537
newellhousemuseum@centurytel.net
www.newellhouse.com

From I-5, take exit 278 toward Champoeg State Park. The house is on the left before you turn into the park's main entrance.

For those of us who like all things historical, the Robert Newell House is the perfect place to enjoy two important jewels of the past … traditional teatime and an historic home. Owned by the Daughters of the Revolution, the home is a beautiful reminder of how things used to be, just as tea time is a reminder of what can be ... a slower, gentler time. If you plan to visit the museum, invite a group of friends and enjoy an afternoon of tea and conversation in this wonderfully preserved 1850's farmhouse.

There are a number of different teas available ranging in price from the $14 Princess Tea which consists of tea, scones, and fruit to The Royal Tea which offers tea, 3 tea sandwiches, 2 savories, scone w/jam and clotted cream, fresh fruit and dessert for $22. The prices are for a minimum of 10 and include admission to tour the house. During the summer, teas may be held in the garden, on Rebecca's Tea Porch or in the Great Room. During inclement weather teas are presented in the Great Room or on Rebecca's Tea Porch only. We had the pleasure of taking tea inside and it was such a perfect setting - seated at antique tables covered with vintage linens and wonderful old mismatched china cups and saucers, surrounded by so many remnants of the past. Tea was served in courses and iced tea as well as hot tea was included.

During the course of the afternoon, our hostess, Judy, gave a detailed history of the house and its relationship to the town of Champoeg. After a leisurely tea, we were able to ramble about the house taking in all the history it had to offer. How I loved the temporary exhibit of inaugural dresses of former governors' wives that dated back to the 1850's. To top off your visit, take a tour of the grounds and see the jail and school house that have been moved to the property.

Cash/Checks
Wheelchair Accessible on the Porch
Lot Parking

Tea is by appointment only. A two-week deposit is required as is a 48-hour cancellation notice.

Proprietors
Autograph_____Date_____

Our Daily Bread Restaurant

88170 Territorial Road
Veneta, Oregon 97487
541-935-4921
tastefulinquiry@ourdailybreadrestaurant.com
www.ourdailybreadrestaurant.com

From Eugene, take Hwy 126 to Veneta, about a 12 minute drive. Turn left on Territorial Hwy. They are located on the corner of Territorial Hwy and E. Broadway Avenue.

Our Daily Bread is housed in a beautifully renovated country church with white washed walls, hardwood floors, high ceilings and stained glass windows. The owner, Tabitha Eck, who opened the business in 1985, has decorated the interior in burgundy and adjusts with the seasons and themes of the teas.

Afternoon Tea is served tableside or as a buffet. It includes an assortment of finger sandwiches, mini pastries, mini desserts and a pot of tea for $12.95 per person. There is a 15-person minimum. The Children's Tea has black tea or lemonade, PB & J mini sandwiches, celery & peanut butter boats, deviled egg friendly faces, gingerbread people and chocolate cupcakes. Finally, the High Tea is a 3-course tea served tableside or as a buffet and it offers mini pastries, cookies, desserts, fresh fruit, cheeses or meats and finger sandwiches plus a pot of their hot organic tea. Scones served with clotted cream and preserves can be added for .75 each. An additional course can be added for $2 more. The bakery will help you design just the perfect menu for your group. The initial cost is $23.95 per person and there is a 15 person minimum.

The menu includes a full service restaurant which serves breakfast, lunch, dinner and a Sunday brunch. They also offer catering and on-site banquets.

MC/V/DEB/DIS
Wheelchair Accessible
Lot and Street Parking

Tea is by appointment only. There is a 3 day cancellation policy.

Proprietors
Autograph_____Date_____

Ruthie B's Tea Room

346 Main Street
Springfield, Oregon 97477
541-988-4791

From I-5, take exit 194A to City Center Exit. Turn right on Pioneer Parkway to Main Street. Turn left on Main then left again on 4th Street. They are on the corner next to Econo Sales.

This is so much more than a tea room! Ruth describes her tea room as "Fun with Tea and Art" and that is an understatement. The ambience ranges from Vintage to Primitive, from Mid-century to Contemporary. Whatever your passion, you will be able to satisfy it here.

The massive room is divided into 28 "rooms" which are separated by antiques and collectibles. The 28 tables are each is set for 4-8 people. You have the opportunity to shop from your seat, as temptation is all around you.

Once you are seated, your server brings glasses of water, then scatters lavender on the table and blows bubbles to lighten the moment. The service is fun and efficient, and your order is taken in a timely manner.

There are two tea sets to choose from: The Garden Tea includes your tea of choice, soup, 4 tea sandwiches, 2 savory salads and shortbread treats for $16 or High Tea which starts with your tea of choice and a warm scone topped with Devonshire clotted cream and fresh Oregon berry jam. This is followed by a cup of Ruth's famous creamy tomato basil soup. Then, the main course of 4 assorted tea sandwiches and two savory salads are presented. Finally, cranberry compote will cleanse your palate and prepare you for the six bite sized desserts that complete this tea which is offered for $22 per person.

Themed teas, including an Alice In Wonderland Tea, are available by request. They are offered only with Hi Tea or the Garden Tea. There is a children's menu which offers all of the kid's favorites … to big and little kids!

If you wish to have something other than tea items, the menu offers numerous other specialties – vb jquiche, mac 'n cheese, hot and cold sandwiches, salads and more. There is something for everyone.

Just remember, when you arrive, plan for a very long visit! This is a very interesting place!

MC/V/DEB/DIS/Checks
Wheelchair Accessible
Street Parking

Hours of operation are Tuesday through Saturday 10-4. The last tea service is at 4. Reservations for tea are required 24 hours in advance.

Proprietors
Autograph_____Date_____

SerendipiTea Tea Room

4660 S.E. Highway 101
Lincoln City, Oregon 97367
541-996-2200
steaminstina@earthlink.net
www.serendipitea.net

Located on Hwy 101 about ½ mile south of The Inn at Spanish Head. Enter the Taft Chevron parking lot and the tea house is on the right. They are across the street from the Bank of the West.

Owner Stina Seeger-Gibson opened her tea room in 2008 and by doing so added one more "attraction" to Lincoln City. Located in the area called Taft, this interesting building offers one a number of locations in which to take tea. There is the intimate room for two, the group area which seats 8 or the main dining room which includes fireside tables. Done in shades of soothing pink and lavender, the rooms are comfortable and cozy. Soft classical music fills the room and an assortment of beautiful antiques completes the feeling of being in a very special place. Tea tables are set with china tea cups and saucers from Stina's extensive collection, soft lavender tablecloths, fresh flowers and beautiful silver.

The tea choices start with the traditional cream tea which is called a Spot of Tea. Just Enough offers a pot of tea, a plate of sandwiches, a scone and a dessert, and Tecla's Tea, named in honor of Stina's Norwegian grandmother, consists of a pot of tea and a selection of delightful desserts. The above teas are priced at $12. For $14 one may choose the Afternoon Tea which includes a pot of tea, sorbet, savories, sweet and savory scones, tea sandwiches and desserts, all served on a tiered server. Finally, the SerendipiTea High Tea is presented on a tiered server which is laden with a larger portion of the above treats along with a pot of tea for $19. All teas include lemon curd, jam and clotted cream. For the younger set the Moppet's Tea is offered for $9 and it has sorbet, sandwiches, scones and desserts as well as a pot of tea.

After taking your leisurely tea, be sure to allow time to browse the extensive gift area in the front of the shop. You are sure to find something to take home for yourself or a friend. I did!

MC/V/DEB/CASH
Wheelchair Accessible
Parking Lot

Tea times are Wednesday through Sunday, 11-5. Reservation suggested for groups of 4 or more. There is a $3 per plate charge for shared menu items.

Proprietors
Autograph_____Date_____

Shelton-McMurphey-Johnson House

303 Willamette Street
Eugene, Oregon 97401
541-484-0808
fax 541-984-1413
director@smjhouse.org
www.smjhouse.org

From I-5, take Eugene/U of O exit over the Ferry Street Bridge. Go right on 3rd. and follow directions to Pearl Street. The house is located off 3rd and Pearl.

This is the perfect location for afternoon tea ... a stately Victorian mansion located in the heart of Eugene. The Shelton-McMurphey-Johnson House offers specialty teas in honor of Valentine's Day, Mother's Day and Christmas. The traditional high tea menu offers tea, scones, a variety of tea sandwiches, and a selection of decadent desserts. The tea offerings are catered in by some of the areas finest caterers and cost $25 per person. Since these teas are very popular, they fill up quickly, so plan ahead and make reservations well in advance.

Private teas may be scheduled for groups of 6 to 35 for $15 per person and are available only by prior arrangement. This tea includes tea, a scone, two tea sandwiches, a dessert and a sweet treat. You bring the group and SMJ House provides the ambience and food!

Both specialty and private teas include a tour of the historic house. Allow yourself time to take the tour of this beautiful reminder of our elegant past. It is quite large and well worth your time.

Visa/MC
Cash/Checks
Wheelchair Accessible
Lot Parking

Specialty teas are offered in February, May and December. Advance reservations are required and there is a cancellation policy. Private teas for groups of 6-35 people are also available.

Proprietors
Autograph_____Date_____

Sister Act Party Specialists

Catering & Teas
Corvallis, Oregon 97330
541-752-7624
541-757-6525
jacobt@peak.org

Alicia and Deanna cater off-site, at your home or other location of your choice.

As the name implies, Alicia and Deanna are sisters and they have a broad background in the catering business. They started at an early age, helping their mother with her catering business, and then ventured out on their own when they became mothers themselves.

Though they do all types of catering, presenting teas is a favorite activity. This duo has done a tea for as few as two people and as many as seventy-five. A typical afternoon tea includes sandwiches, savories, fruit, scones with Devonshire cream, lemon curd and jam, assorted desserts and, of course, tea. Some of their special tea items are tomato and fresh basil on crostini, egg salad pocket, rotisserie chicken wrap, ham and asparagus roll, Florentine square and their signature bacon ranch pinwheel.

Other types of teas are available depending on your needs, and price is dependent on what type of tea you choose. The average range is $10 to $15. They also enjoy doing theme teas such as Mother's Day, Valentine's Day, Christmas, Birthday Parties, Bridal and Baby Showers as well as your personal theme choice. Teas for children are of special interest to these moms, and the tea features peanut butter and jelly sandwiches, meat/cheese stacks, shaped cheese sandwiches, fruit, mini cupcakes, cookies and a party favor for $6.50 to $8. Additional items which they would be happy to provide for a minimal fee are linens, tableware, teapots and other tea accoutrements, dishes, and decorations.

Besides teas, Sister Act does catering for groups and individuals at the client's home or at another location. Call for prices and specific information.

One-week notice on teas is appreciated.

Proprietor
Autograph_____Date_____

Society Woman

8855 S.W. Holly Lane. Suite 121
Wilsonville, Oregon 97070
503-582-0646
Sharon.arnett@thesocietywoman.com
www.thesocietywoman.com

Take exit 183 (from north turn left on Wilsonville Road; from South turn right on Wilsonville Road) then turn right on Parkway (first turn after you exit the freeway). Turn left on Holly Lane and immediately turn left into the parking lot.

This is the ultimate Red Hat store, where you sit for awhile and enjoy one of Sharon Arnett's custom-made teas ... then shop 'til you drop! Or if you prefer ... shop first! Then you can share your treasures during tea.

For $16 per person, not including gratuity, you may enjoy one of Sharon's three tea selections. The menu changes three times a year and you can check out the website to get the current choices. Recent selections included the Mermaid Luncheon which offered tea, cheese ball with cracker plate, clam chowder , shrimp salad and Pineapple Hula, and the Lemon Twist which included lemon tea, lemon poppy seed scone with lemon curd, white chili soup, croissant chicken salad sandwich and lemon bars. The High Tea, which is served on tiered servers, had a tea assortment, fresh blueberry scones, fruit and crackers, assorted finger sandwiches and cheese cake. You may also purchase tea and scones or dessert for $5 or tea only for $1.50 per person.

Groups of up to 24 can be accommodated. You may stay as little or as long as you would like and enjoy the ambience in a 100% Red Hat store.

Cash/Checks/V
Wheelchair Accessible
Lot Parking

The store is open Tuesday through Saturday from 10 to 5. Teas are by reservation and are served between 11 and 3.

Proprietors
Autograph_____Date_____

Stratford House

Stratford House

203 E. Main Street
Hillsboro, Oregon 97123
503-648-7139
Stratford_House@Verizon.net

From I-5, take exit 292 toward Beaverton (Hwy 217). Take the ramp onto US-26 (Sunset Highway). At exit 65, keep right onto the ramp. Turn left onto Cornell. Bear right onto E. Main Street.

This is one of the many tea rooms appropriately located in the historic district of town where renovations have drawn people back to the community's roots. Stratford House, owned by Steve and Alice Stratford, was opened in 2000. It dwells in one of the old buildings where brick and wood, high ceilings and deep rooms set the tone for a trip back to the past. A recessed entryway, set off by double-sided display windows, greets you. The tea room shares space with an antiques business, so one is surrounded with history in the form of furnishings, decorations, clothing, linens and household items from yester-year. The area where tea is served reminds one of an old-fashioned soda fountain. The counter is on one wall, and an array of tables, covered with linens and lace, fills the room.

The tea set is presented on tiered-servers and tea comes in mismatched pots. None of the teacups and saucers come from the same set. It is fun to see the wonderful variety of china pieces!

The High Tea, which requires a pre-paid reservation, offers tea sandwiches, fruit, scones with Devon cream and lemon curd, petite desserts and a pot of tea. A Cream Tea is available as well as a Tea Plate which offers soup, sandwich and petite dessert. The last two teas are offered anytime. A Princess Tea for the little ones is available in their own area with their own tea table.

Besides tea, Stratford House offers light breakfast items including a breakfast sandwich special. Quiche, sandwiches and soup may be purchased for lunch. Alice's signature soup, Hungarian mushroom, brings customers back again and again! A variety of hot and cold beverages is also available.

V/MC/Checks
Wheelchair Accessible
Free Street Parking

High Tea is by reservation only. The shop is open from 8 to 4.

Proprietors
Autograph_____Date_____

Tas Tea

Loose Leaf Tea

425 S.W. Madison Avenue, Suite D
Corvallis, Oregon 97330
541-753-4017
bethpowell@tas-tea.com
www.tas-tea.com

From Hwy 34, come over the bridge and make a left turn onto 4th Street. They are on the corner of 4th and Madison, in the Starbucks building.

Though not a full service tea room, Tas Tea is a wonderful retail shop specializing in a large selection of loose leaf teas. It is the perfect place to stop for a cup of piping hot tea or a glass of brewed ice tea. The owner, Beth, purchased the already successful tea shop in 2006, and she has worked diligently to learn all she can about our favorite beverage. She certainly has mastered the brewing of a perfect cup!

The shop is small but roomy and there are a couple of comfortable chairs with adjacent tables for taking a break to enjoy your cuppa. The tea choices include Special Teas, The Jasmine Pearl and of course, the Tas Tea line.

Should you be looking for a special gift for a friend, or if you are seeking to add to your collection of tea accoutrements, Beth has many lovely gifts in her tea shop. I've had my eye on a cute frog tea pot for some time. I am sure it will make its way into my collection! Besides tea pots, you may be interested in tea cups, strainers, books and other items available for purchase. Be sure to ask Beth to demonstrate her Smart Strainer while you are there.

MC/V/AE/DEB/DIS/Checks
Wheelchair Accessible
Street Parking, some Metered

The shop is open Monday through Saturday from 10 to 5.

Proprietors
Autograph_____Date_____

66

The Tea & Herb Shop

Water Street Market
151 N.W. Monroe Street
Corvallis, Oregon 97330
541-752-0283
Theteaandherbshop@earthlink,net

From I-5, take Exit 228 to Corvallis (Hwy 34). Go 10 miles and cross the bridge into town and take a left at 2nd Street. Take a left at Monroe, and The Water Street Market is on the corner of Monroe and1st Streets.

This business has been in this location since June 2005. Water Street Market was completed in 2005 and houses a number of food oriented businesses - a restaurant, a fish market that also sells gourmet foods, a wine store and more. Tucked into a corner of the market is this wonderful gem, which is owned by Peggy Leedberg. Peggy sells an extensive and interesting selection of teas and herbs.

The shop is small but comfortable, and well laid out. An abundance of windows keeps the room light and cheerful. One long wall holds shelves of large glass jars filled with fragrant loose leaf teas. Many of them are organic and fair trade. Behind the counter there are shelves that hold a nice selection of herbs.

Peggy offers teas from China, Japan, Kenya, India, Ceylon, Taiwan and South Africa. She also has many blended teas. The selection includes black, oolong, pu-erh, green, white, herbals, Rooibos and other teas. The teas are sold by the ounce and range in price from $1.30 to $10 per ounce. You can also get a cup of your favorite tea to go.

Besides teas, Peggy has a nice selection of tea accoutrements from strainer to pots.

Cash/Checks
Wheelchair Accessible
Lot and Metered Street Parking

Hours of operation are Thursday and Friday 11-6, Saturday 10-6 and Sunday 1-5.

Proprietors
Autograph_____Date_____

Tea Events

P.O. Box 7102
Bend, Oregon 97708
541-279-1023
www.StartATeaBusiness.com
www.TeaEvents.com

Dawnya Sasse is the creative force behind Tea Events, a tea business training company. Tea Events offers a variety of programs aimed at training new tea entrepreneurs in the tea business of their dreams. Tea Events flagship program, "Start a Tea Business" ™, offers complete on-line tea business training from the comfort of your own home.

The "Start a Tea Business"™ class offers students a firm foundation in tea concepts, tea cupping, tea history, business planning and in-depth education on 17 different types of tea-related businesses. Everything you need to begin in the tea industry is available in this class, including inside information on over 200 wholesalers longing for your business.

Dawnya Sasse is a highly trained tea professional, beginning in the tea industry in 1997 during its "pioneer days." She has successfully owned and operated a British tea room and a by-reservations tea room (for 7 years), led British Tea Tours and trained hundreds of students on-line and in person. Dawnya has been educated by a Who's Who in the tea industry including Pearl Dexter, James Norwood Pratt, Jennifer Peterson, Ron and Donna Lasko, Tomislov Podreka, Bill Waddington, Richard Gusauska, Elizabeth Knight and Edward Brahma of the Brahma Tea Museum in London, England. She has received numerous certificates from programs all over the world.

Dawnya has also been featured in numerous publications including; The Country Register, The Gilded Lily, The Teahouse Times, Tea Experiences, The Bend Bulletin, The Vancouver Columbian and The Saint Louis Post-Dispatch.

For more information on her tea classes both on-line
and in person, be sure to visit:

www.TeaEvents.com and
www.StartATeabusiness.com

Proprietors
Autograph_____Date_____

The Tea Parlour

664 Greenwood Street
Junction City, Oregon 97448
541-998-8775

From Hwy 99, drive through Junction City and turn east on 6th Street then turn left on Greenwood Street. They are across from the Post Office and next door to the Police Station.

Opened in 2008 by Debbie Horn, this little tea room is just what Junction City needed. Located close to so many other communities, this will become a destination for those of us who appreciate that respite known as "tea time." The saying that wraps around the room says it all, "A cup of tea shared … is happiness tasted … and time well spent."

The décor is contemporary yet a bit retro. The color scheme is pink and black with touches of white. The five small square tables are accompanied by black chairs and are decked out with white linen cloths and black cloth napkins. The tea cozies, in assorted patterns of pink and black, keep the tea hot in the dainty white teapots. A large picture window completes the warm and open feeling in this special little tea room.

Black racks and cupboards are laden with gifts, many of which are pink and black. Bulk tea is available for purchase, also. The seating capacity is 20 persons and reservations are required.

The tea sets range from Tea & Scones for $5.50 to the Full Tea for $15. Tea & Sweets is offered for $6.50 and tea & Savories is $7.50. The Full Tea menu changes monthly and consists of savories, 2 scones, sweets and a pot of tea. Other beverage choices are hot chocolate and pink strawberry lemonade. All drinks are refillable.

After tea, a walk about Junction City is in order. There are many small stores and curiosity shops to idle away a couple of hours.

Handicapped Accessible
Street Parking

The tea room is open Tuesday through Friday from 11-5 and on Saturday from 11-4.

Proprietors
Autograph_____Date_____

The Tea Party

716 N.W. Beach Drive
Newport, Oregon 97365
541-574-0545 / 877-T-Party7
info@theteapartycompany.com
www.theteapartycompany.com

From the Hwy 20/Hwy 101 intersection, go west to Coast Street. Turn right on Coast then left on Beach. You will be at the turn-around in Historic Nye Beach. The tall Tudor building on the right is your destination.

A bright yellow door welcomes you to this tea room which is located in a Tudor style building in Historic Nye Beach. It was opened in 2005 by Clair McNeely and her daughter Lucinda Chapman. Once inside you will see windows adorned with soft miniature floral yellow curtains with yellow plaid tie-backs. The plaid pattern is carried out on the half-wall room divider just inside the door. A charming bench in the gift area is provided for those waiting to be seated. Speaking of gifts, the selection is interesting and extensive. Be sure to allow yourself time to shop!

For tea, the selections begin with a Scone Plate for $4.50. Sweet Delights which includes sorbet and six dainty sweets, and Soup and Savories are both available for $9.50. The Classic Tea offers sorbet, four finger sandwiches, two hot savories, a scone with all the fixings and three small desserts for $16.95. Savory Delights is much like the Classic Tea except that the sweets are replaced with 4 additional finger sandwiches and savories for $16.95. All teas include a pot of tea, and all the fixings for the scones. All hot teas may be served with a glass of ice as well. Special dietary needs may be accommodated with prior arrangements. For guests 12 and under, there is a seasonally themed Mad Hatter Tea for $6.95. It includes sorbet, a peanut butter and jelly sandwich, cookie, fruit and a beverage.

Coffee is available as well as lavender lemonade, hot chocolate and Italian sodas. Champagne and Oregon wines may be purchased for $6. Food-To-Go for parties or groups can be purchased but you must pick it up.

In 2008, Claire and Lucinda opened their Bed and Breakfast which is on the 2nd floor of the building. There are 3 rooms to choose from, each with its own bath. The use of their parlor and patio is included.. You can look at the rooms on their website and you can call 541-574-0545 to book your vacation.

V/MC/AE/DEB/DIS
Wheelchair Accessible
Street Parking

The tea room opens on Friday and Saturday at 11 a.m. and on Sunday at noon. The last tea service is at 2:30. Reservations are strongly recommended as they can be very busy! Groups are welcome.

Proprietors
Autograph_____Date_____

The Tea Zone

510 N.W. 11th Avenue
Portland, Oregon 97209
503-221-2130
teazone@teazone.com
www.teazone.com

I-5 to 405 N (299B) and take exit 2B to Everett Street. The exit will merge onto 14th Avenue. Follow 14th about 4 blocks to Hoyt Street and turn right. Go to 11th Street and turn left. The shop is on the left side.

Located in the historic Pearl District, The Tea Zone offers over 90 loose-leaf teas, bearing their own label, and ranging in price from $2.50 to $8 per ounce. There are also some specialty teas and artisan teas which are individually priced. If you are looking for prepared tea, it can be purchased at $3.75-4.75 for a one-person pot and $5.75 to $7.75 for a two-person pot.

With the addition of the Camellia Lounge, they now offer wine, beer, and tea infused cocktails along with tea lattes and tea tonics, and they were voted Portland's best Bubble Teas. The Camellia Lounge has live music at night and offers a range of appetizers. To accompany your beverage, you can purchase scones (they say the best in town!), tarts, cookies, desserts and other treats.

This European-style establishment also offers hardier fare, and the choices are numerous. They include empanadas, salads, soup, quiche, grilled panini sandwiches and a Southwest tuna sandwich. These entrées range in price from $3.75 to $8.95 and a mixed greens side salad may be added for $2.25. Daily specials are also available. When possible, dietary needs can be accommodated.

For those of us who enjoy the event called "Tea Time," monthly High Teas, excluding summer months and Holiday High Teas are offered.

MC/V/AE/DIS/Checks
Wheelchair Accessible
Metered Street Parking
Self-Serve Pay Lot is Available

Weekdays open at 8 a.m., weekends open at 10 a.m. Sunday and Monday closed at 7 p.m. Tuesday to Saturday they close at midnight. Call for dates and times of High Tea. They are offered the three weeks prior to Christmas.

Proprietors
Autograph_____Date_____

Teas Me

23855 S.W. 195th Place
Sherwood, Oregon 97140
503-625-1929
julie@teasme.net
www.teasme.net

Located off 99W between Sherwood and Newberg, the exit is 3/4 miles south of the Sherwood YMCA. Go 1/4 mile west on Chapman Road. Follow green Hwy signs to "Sleighbells."

The owner, Julie Epperson, calls her tea room British Style with a Northwest flair! The tea room, with its dark red walls and fun art work was opened by Julie in 2006. It is located in a corner of Sleighbells, the renowned Christmas store. Outside on the property, you can get a great view of Mt. Hood and enjoy the sight of peacocks, turkeys, chickens and rabbits. Inside the building, you can shop the huge "red barn" before and after taking afternoon tea.

The themes for the tea menu change monthly and you can find them on their website. An example would be July, which was called a Red, White & Blue Theme Menu. The Liberty Tea featured sorbet, 2 scones, a savory, 3 finger sandwiches, cream cheese tartlet, fresh fruit and 3 dessert sweets for $19.95. The Freedom Tea offered sorbet, 2 scones, 3 finger sandwiches, fresh fruit and 2 desserts sweets for $15.95. Finally, the Stars & Stripes Tea included sorbet, 1 scone, 2 finger sandwiches, fresh fruit and 2 dessert sweets for $12.95. Fresh baked scones are served hot with real imported English clotted cream and handmade English sweet curds and jam. All three tea sets include a pot of tea and the featured teas for July were Red Rooibos, White Lightning and Blueberry. During the summer sorbet is included, but soup is available in lieu of sorbet or soup can be purchased as an extra.

Catering is available and there is a banquet room which can accommodate up to 75 guests. They also offer menu specials which may peak your interest.

There is a nice gift area with tea accoutrements and specialty foods. They also retail their teas. This is a great destination and is well worth the drive, so plan to spend the day.

MC/V/DEB/DIS/Checks
Handicapped Accessible
Parking Lot

Hours of operation are Thursday through Monday from 11:30 to 4 and reservations are preferred. The last tea service is at 3:30. Holiday teas are offered. Groups are welcome with advance reservations. For October through December, reservations need to be made well in advance. There is a 24 hour cancellation policy.

Proprietors
Autograph___*Julie Epperson*___ Date_12-14-09_

Thank You!

Windsor House of Tea

1044 Marine Drive
Astoria, Oregon 97103
503-338-6900
www.thewindsorhouseoftea.com

From west on Hwy 30, which becomes Marine Drive in Astoria, go to 10th Street. The tea room is on the right side of the street. From Hwy 101, which becomes Commercial, proceed through town to the downtown area. Turn left on 11th then left on Marine. The tearoom is on the right side of the street.

In 2004, Shirley George and Susan Windsor Widawski opened their tea room in the completely renovated Sanborn Building located on the corner of 10th and Marine Dr. In 2006 the tea room moved to larger accommodations in the Sanborn Building, conveniently located on street level. The interior of the tea room, with its eclectic tables and chairs, tea sets and dishes, antiques and colorful linens is large enough to accommodate parties up to 50 people. It has a "dress up" room for children's tea party events, a large gift shop located at the entrance to the tea room and a separate tea bar where you can get tea and scones to go. The gift shop sells over 60 varieties of loose leaf specialty tea, selected gifts and tea accessories and accoutrements.

The menu in the tea room offers traditional teas sets including the Lady Taylor's Tea for $6.95 which features scones with Devonshire cream, lemon curd and jam. The Windsor Tea for $7.95 is a dessert tea. The next selection is a Ploughman's Plate, and it includes a cup of tea, scone or finger sandwiches and a sweet dessert for $8.95. The Queen's Tea is $10.95 and it offers sorbet, miniature quiches, a scone with Devonshire cream, lemon curd and jam, and a selection of desserts. Finally, there is the Royal High Tea which starts with a trio of sorbets, followed by a tiered server of sweets and savories consisting of a variety of finger sandwiches, two scones with Devonshire cream, lemon curd and jam, and ending with a selection of desserts for $16.95. All teas include a pot of tea, perhaps their house brand Metropolitan-Windsor Castle. Some dietary needs may be accommodated with prior arrangements. For children, Sir Aidan's Tea includes finger sandwiches of peanut butter and jelly and cheese, fruit, cookies and choice of hot chocolate or apple juice for $6.95.

C/V/AE/DEB/DIS
Wheelchair Accessible
On-Street Parking

The tea room is open Tuesday through Saturday 11-4 and the Gift Shop is open 10-5. They are closed Sunday and Monday. Any time is tea time. Reservations are appreciated. The tea room is available for special events.

Proprietors
Autograph_____Date_____

Welcome
to
Washington

A Touch of Elegance

508 W. Bell Lane
Saint John, Washington 99171
509-648-3466
www.barbkile.com

Saint John is approximately 55 miles south of Spokane. From Hwy 195, turn west on Steptoe and go 14 miles. Turn south on Saint John Endicott Road, go 2 short blocks and turn right on Liberty. It becomes Bell Lane at the Catholic Church. They are the last house on the right.

Chintz-covered table cloths and chair backs, and servers in white starched aprons, greet you as you enter this charming Victorian-style tea room. These are some of the special touches that Barb Kite offers to those looking for gracious hospitality for their special event. Not just a tea room, but also a place to have a memorable luncheon with friends and family.

A catered lunch consists of two menu items of your choice: soup, salad or dessert, with sorbet and bread, for $20 per person including tax. If you choose to have soup, salad, bread and dessert, the cost is $25. With so many soups, salad and bread choices, selecting one will be a challenge! Everything is made from scratch by Barb.

Tea time, which is served in a gracious and elegant setting, offers a wonderful Victorian Tea that includes fresh from the oven scones, heart-shaped sandwiches, chicken tartlets, heart-shaped cheeses, sorbet, truffle, lemon curd tart, chocolate caramel cookie, triple chocolate mousse, carrot cake and seasonal desserts. Assorted jams and jellies, spun honey butter and Devon cream are served with the scones. The desserts are garnished with Barb's signature chocolate lace butterfly and all this is available for $25, including tax. Special themed teas are offered for holidays and birthdays and special dietary needs can be accommodated upon advance notice. Coffee is available.

Barb has been a florist for over 30 years and she makes all of her beautiful floral decorations and door wreaths. They add a special touch to tea.

After dining, guests are invited to browse through the Creative Workshop Boutique which features gifts, bulk teas and fine furnishings.

Cash/Checks
Not Wheelchair Accessible
Street & Lot Parking

Open 11-5 Monday through Saturday. Tea time is 11-3. Reservations are required 1 week in advance. Holidays require 2 weeks. Groups of 6-24 require a one-week cancellation. You are responsible for the number reserved unless cancellation is made 48-hours in advance.

Proprietors
Autograph_____Date_____

Abbey Garden Tea Room

1312-11th Street
Bellingham, Washington 98225
360-752-1752
www.abbeygardentea.com

From I-5 North - take the Fairhaven Exit and turn left. Turn right at 2nd light (12th Street). Go 2 blocks to light (Harris Street). Turn left, go 1 block then turn left onto 11th Street. You will be in the Fairhaven Historic District.

In 2005, Anne Winfrey moved her tea room next door to a beautiful new building which blends perfectly into the Historic Fairhaven District. Here the tearoom shares space with "Creativitea," a paint-your-own pottery studio offering glass fusing and a tea bar. This "British inspired" tea room is now on the street level. The new décor offers rich mahogany wainscoting, brown velvet chairs, gold curtains and burgundy tablecloths with white runners. Anne uses a wonderful assortment of mismatched china, and the tables are adorned with seasonal fresh flowers. Besides the main tea room, there is an upstairs mezzanine where catered parties may be held.

There are numerous tea sets to choose from: the Cream Tea for $8.95; Abbey Tea of scone, 3 tea sandwiches and fresh fruit for $11.95; Savory Tea with 3 tea sandwiches, choice of quiche, sausage roll or pastry and fresh fruit for $13.95; Afternoon Tea which includes 3 tea sandwiches, choice of dessert and fresh fruit for $12.95; Gentleman's Tea of 3 double tea sandwiches, choice of quiche, sausage roll or pastry and dessert choice for $15.95; and High Tea which includes raspberry or lemon sorbet, 3 tea sandwiches, sausage roll, quiche or pastry, dessert choice and fresh fruit for $18.95. All teas include an individual pot of tea, and scones are served with cream and jam. For children, Anne offers the Lil' Tea which includes 3 tea sandwiches, assorted tea cookies or mini lemon tart and a pot of tea or cocoa for $8.95.

Anne offers over 30 types of tea, both British brands and their own label, which may be purchased in bulk, and coffee is available. Lunch items such as soup, sandwiches, salads and savories are priced from $4.95 to $10.95. Delicious desserts are available for $4.95.

MC/V/Local Checks Only
Wheelchair Accessible
Free Street Parking and a Shared Lot

Tea is served Tuesday through Sunday 11-6. The last seating is at 4:30. Closed Monday and holidays. Reservations are not required. They offer party contracts for catered affairs and an upstairs party room is available.

Proprietors
Autograph_____Date_____

All About Tea

Cyrilla Gleason
360-690-1811
cyrilla.gleason@gmail.com
www.allabouttea.net

*The location for the program, class or workshop will be
determined at the time of booking.*

Cyrilla Gleason is a trained and certified Tea Etiquette Consultant and is the founder
and director of All About Tea, a company specializing in tea education and etiquette.
Programs, classes and workshops are customized to the needs of the client. Mrs. Gleason
has a BA in education and is a certified teacher. She is a member of the Colonial
Williamsburg Foundation and is a graduate of the Protocol School of Washington in
McLean, Virginia, the leader in etiquette and protocol services.

All About Tea programs and workshops provide an entertaining way to learn about
taking tea in business and social situations. As Mrs. Gleason states, "taking tea provides a
special opportunity to spend quality time with friends, family, and associates." Programs
include the history of tea, the proper preparation of tea, and the etiquette used while
taking tea. Antique tea items and new tea accessories are demonstrated in their use of
preparing tea. You will learn how to make the perfect cup of Green, Oolong, and Black
Tea, and why correctly prepared tea never tastes bitter. Programs and classes may be held
in tea shops, businesses, clubs, schools, churches or homes.

Samples of programs are Victorian Tea Traditions, Colonial Days, Mother and
Daughter Tea & Etiquette, Young Men's Manners, and Teddy Bear or Fairy Princess Tea
and Etiquette. Business Etiquette and Tea programs are for professional groups. There is
also a program for church and civic organizations which is perfect for brunch, lunch, tea
or dinner meetings and can be given with or without a devotional.

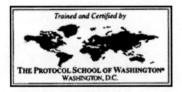

*For more information or to arrange a program, call or email Cyrilla. Classes are
pre-arranged by reservation.*

Proprietors
Autograph_____Date_____

All the Tea & China Tea Room

115-S 2nd Avenue S.W. # B
Ilwaco, Washington 98624
360-642-1345

From the south, take Hwy 101 and cross the Astoria Bridge. Drive 12 miles to Ilwaco. In Ilwaco, pass through the light at 1st. Street. Turn left on 2nd and go one block. The tearoom is on the right. From the north, take Hwy 101 toward the Long Beach Peninsula. Turn left to go to Ilwaco (101-Pacific Hwy Jct.) Turn right at the light and go one block. Turn left and go 1 block to the tearoom.

Located on the Long Beach Peninsula, this charming tea room is a wonderful addition to the town of Ilwaco. The façade is amazing with its bold color, cottage style doors and windows, and well-placed plants and flowers. The interior of the tearoom features eclectic tables & chairs, linens and china of every description, and great art work on the walls. There are gifts and collectibles set about the two rooms on vintage furniture and shelves. There is a lovely sitting area with comfortable stuffed chairs and lot tables for an intimate tea experience. The room has a very warm and cozy atmosphere, perfect for taking tea.

There are two teas to choose from with the smaller one, called Elevensies, offering a pot of fresh tea or coffee and fresh baked scones with fruit for $7 The Iris Afternoon Tea is available for $19.95 and it includes an ever changing assortment of savories, tea sandwiches, scones, breads, fruit and sweets. It comes with a bottomless pot of tea. Share it with a friend for $23.95 and receive additional sandwiches and another pot of tea.

A number of lighter fare items are also on the menu from Susie's Salad, which is a meal in itself, for $9.95 to Jenny's Choice for $12.95. This lunch item includes a sandwich or a selection of tea sandwiches, a scone, fruit and dessert. Marguerite's Garden is a dinner salad of fresh greens accompanied by a sandwich or tea sandwiches and dessert for $10.50 and For Letty offers soup of the day and either a sandwich or tea sandwiches and dessert also for $10.50. The choices are numerous, the presentation beautiful and the meal generous.

For the children, moms can choose Miss Mooney's Tea. It includes whimsical tea sandwiches, fruit, sweets and other finger foods, plus a pint-sized tea pot of pink organic tea, lemonade, cocoa or milk and is priced at $7.50.

Wheelchair Accessible
Lot Parking

They are open Wednesday through Saturday from 11 to 4. Reservations are recommended.

Proprietors
Autograph_____Date_____

Attic Secrets Café & Tea

4229-76th Street N.E., Suite 101
Marysville, Washington 98270
360-659-7305
admin@atticsecrets.com
www.atticsecrets.com

I-5 to exit 200. From the north turn left, go to State Avenue, turn right, and go to 76th (light). Turn left, its 1/2 block on the left side. From the south, same except turn right at exit.

This is Snohomish County's oldest tea room and was voted "Best Place to Dine" by the Everett Herald., as well as, Best Tea Room for 3 years, 2005-2007. Owners Happi and Rick, who purchased the tea room in 1998, refer to the ambience as "Hollywood Romantic," and each of the three rooms is decorated in a different style. All are beautifully appointed with all the finishing touches!

The tea offerings are numerous. The Grand Lady Tea consists of a scone, four tea sandwiches and a specialty dessert, the Serenity Tea features a scone, three tea sandwiches and assorted sweets, the Afternoon Tea offers a scone, sweets and fruit and finally the Peaceful Tea has a choice of 4 or 6 tea sandwiches and a sweet. All of the above include tea and there are 35 tea selections to choose from. Children can enjoy the Little Darling Tea, and children's birthday parties are welcome. Holiday and theme teas are offered throughout the year. Dietary needs can be accommodated with advance notice.

A full lunch menu is available all day and take out is available. Limited catering is also offered.

There is a charming gift shop and tea items, including bulk tea, are offered.

MC/V/DIS
Wheelchair Accessible
Lot and Street Parking

The shop is open Monday through Friday 10:30-4:30 and Saturday 10:30-4. Tea time is ALL DAY! Reservations are recommended. Walk-ins are welcome, though there may be a short wait. The last tea is served one hour before closing.

Proprietors
Autograph_____Date_____

The Brambleberry Cottage

and Tea Shoppe
206 E. Pacific Avenue
Spokane, Washington 99202
509-926-3293
www.brambleberrycottage.com

From I-90, take the Division Street exit north. Travel 3 blocks to Pacific and turn right. They are located in the third block, second house on the right. The nearest cross street is Cowley.

When you see the wrought iron fence surrounding this 1906 vintage cottage, you know you have arrived. Flowers, including roses, wisteria, foxglove and hydrangeas welcome you to this charming tea oasis. There are four rooms, each with a different theme, in which to take tea. The Lady Rose Room features writing and roses on the wall; The French Room walls are done in soft green swirls; The News Room has old 30's and 40's newspapers from the cottage and finally there is the Cottage Garden. It will be fun to return frequently and choose the room that suits your mood!

The tea offerings are Tea and Light Refreshments for $15 which includes fruit, scone or crumpet, three finger sandwiches and an elegant dessert, and A Special Tea for $18 which offers fruit, scone or crumpet, and a special sampling of their sandwiches and desserts. Both teas are served on silver tiers. High Tea, which is $22, includes fruit, sandwiches, crumpets, scones and an assortment of desserts. The High Tea is served on an elegant gold tier in grand English tradition. All teas include tea.

The ladies traditionally have a theme tea once a month that consists of an entirely different menu to fit the theme of the tea. Many tea labels are offered including Metropolitan, Market Spice, Montana T & S, and Harney and Sons. Coffee is available and special dietary needs may be requested in advance.

While there, take time to check out the gift and antique area. There are many "must haves" to be sure!

MC/V/Checks
Wheelchair Accessible
Street Parking

Shop hours are Tuesday through Saturday 10-5. Afternoon tea is served Wednesday through Saturday 11-3, by reservation only. Cancel by 9 a.m. the day of the reservation. The tea room can accommodate up to 50 guests.

Proprietors
Autograph_____Date_____

The British Pantry, Ltd.

Bakery, Deli, Restaurant & Gift Shop

8125 - 161st Avenue N.E.
Redmond, Washington 98052
425-883-7511
alvia@thebritishpantryltd.com
www.thebritishpantryltd.com

Go north on 405 to 520. Take the Redmond Way exit and turn left at the light. Proceed to 161st and turn right. Go 1/2 block and the tearoom is on the left in a row of shops. Look for the British flag!

Opened in 1978 by Mavis Redman, the British Pantry celebrated its 30th anniversary in 2008. The business has earned a reputation for good food, friendly service and a wonderful selection of groceries and gift items straight from the United Kingdom. They have been able to provide their traditional British fare to Prince Charles on his return flight from Japan and Prince Phillip on his visit to NW Trek.

If an English afternoon tea room is what you are seeking, you will find it here. Afternoon Tea is offered from 2:30 to 4:30 daily and the set menu consists of cucumber sandwiches, scone with jam and Devon cream, small cake, fresh fruit and house tea for $10.99. We recommend that you allow room for dessert, because the trifle is absolutely wonderful. We started a chain reaction when we ordered it!

The British Pantry shares space with "Nevell's at the British Pantry." The restaurant lunch menu features British favorites such as pasties, sausage rolls, fish and chips and Ploughman's plate, as well as sandwiches, soups and salads. For the sweet tooth, the list is extensive ... trifle, tarts, cheese cake, pies, cakes and much more. For dinner, you may choose from the above as well as other more substantial items - chicken Wellington, roast beef with Yorkshire pudding, bangers & mash, and many more items.

You don't have to be British to enjoy the many offerings in the extensive gift shop, but if you are, the selection from the "mother land" is wonderful. Be sure to allow time to stop here before your departure from the tea room.

Cash/MC/V
Wheelchair Accessible
Lot Parking

The shop is open Monday and Tuesday from 10-6 and Wednesday-Sunday 10-9. Lunch is offered before 4:30. Breakfast is served on Sunday from 10-12. Dinner is served Wednesday-Sunday from 5-9.

Proprietors
Autograph_____Date_____

The Brits

A British Tea Garden & Gift Shoppe

1427 Commerce Avenue
Longview, Washington 98632
360-575-8090

From I-5, take exit 432 and proceed into town. Take a right at 15th then a right on Maple. Go one block and turn right on Commerce. From the Oregon side of the river, cross the bridge and stay on Oregon Way. Turn right on Hudson and left on Commerce.

We were traveling north on one of our tea tours when we stopped in Longview to try this tea room. We were so glad we did! The room, with its distinctive British feel, was warm and inviting. Eclectic tables and chairs, crisp linens, an elevated fireside area and hats galore add to its charm. The new owner, Alice Dietz, purchased the tea room in 2008 and continues to offer the same quality and delicious afternoon tea the previous owner did.

The high tea tables are covered with linens and fine china, and the tea set is presented on tiered servers. The tea menu includes sandwiches, scones, tart, fruit and desserts for $16.95 for adults and $9.95 for children plus gratuity. The scones are delicious, and are accompanied by double Devon cream and very tasty jam. A piping pot of Yorkshire Gold tea is included. There is also a nice selection of lunch items, including many traditional British dishes.

After tea, take time to do a little shopping in the expanded gift area. On one wall there is a nice array of British foods plus a selection of English teas. Beautiful tea pots, as well as cup and saucer sets, are available for purchase along with other tea accoutrements.

This is a wonderful opportunity to take tea as it is offered in traditional English tea rooms.

MC/V/Local Checks
Wheelchair Accessible
Street and Lot Parking

The shop is open 11-3 Monday through Friday. High tea is offered all day by reservation. Saturdays are available for groups of 15 or more.

Proprietors
Autograph_____Date_____

Buster House Tea Room

7th & Main Streets
Pomeroy, Washington 99347
503-843-5009
www.busterhousetearoom.com

Although the tea room just opened in July 2006, the building that houses it has a long and storied history. Located in the Historic Hotel Revere, the original restaurant was opened in 1874 by Martha and Joseph Pomeroy in honor of their son Eugene "Buster" Pomeroy. The Hotel changed names and housed many different businesses over the years before it was vacated from 1978 to 1999. The current owners, John and Beverly Adams-Gordon, purchased the property in 1990 and began its historic restoration. It was listed on the National Register of Historic places in 2004 and the Pomeroy Historic Register in 2007. Decorated in shades of burgundy, dark blue and gold, this is a grand place to take afternoon tea!

The tea selections are numerous, starting with a cream tea for $6.95 and a sweet tea for $8.95. The Afternoon Tea, which offers scones, sandwiches, mini quiche, deviled eggs, fruit garnish and mini desserts, is $18.95. The Edwardian Luncheon Tea, priced at $21.95, includes scones, main dish of the day, greens, fruit garnish and a signature dessert. Finally, there is the Victorian High Tea. This tea, offered at $26.95, includes scones, soup, a tearoom favorite such as chicken divine, quiche or shepherds pie, roll, fruit or sorbet and a signature dessert. All teas include tea and Devonshire cream, preserves and whipped butter. For their younger friends, the Princess Tea is available for $16.95 and it consists of scones, a tea tray of kid-friendly sandwiches, desserts and fruit. The tea starts with dress-up time and a special reading. The birthday "princess" can wear a "real rhinestone" crown and birthday cake can be requested. For the adventurer, the Old Fashioned Picnic Tea can be ordered for $16.95 and it includes a basket, tea set and folding English picnic tea table. Deposit required on the hard items.

On the first Friday of each month, Beverly offers a To-go Luncheon Tea for $9.95. You'll receive a huge gourmet sandwich, scone with toppings, greens and a sweet treat. Iced tea or hot tea is included. You can email them for a copy of the monthly menu. If you're not taking tea in the tea room, Buster house offers Tea and Treats To-go which you can enjoy while browsing the Castlemoyle Books and Gifts, or while seated at one of the indoor tables or their outdoor sidewalk tables, weather permitting. There is something for everyone, and every excuse to stop by for a cuppa or afternoon tea.

V/MC/AE/ Checks
Handicapped Accessible
Street Parking

Hours of operation are 9-5 Monday through Saturday. All teas are by reservation.

Proprietors
Autograph_____Date_____

E.J. Roberts Mansion

W. 1923 First Street
Spokane, Washington 99201
509-456-8839 / 866-456-8839
bob@ejrobertsmansion.com
www.ejrobertsmansion.com

From the north, take the Maple Street bridge route. Take the 1st right at the light after you cross the bridge. Continue straight ahead on 2nd Avenue to Cannon Street. Turn right on Cannon, go to 1st Avenue, and turn right on 1st. The Mansion is on your right.

The E.J. Roberts Mansion, long considered Spokane's best example of Queen Anne architecture, is now open to the public for corporate events, private dinner parties, weddings and Afternoon Tea. The Mansion continues the fine tradition of elaborate entertaining begun by Mrs. Roberts at the turn-of-the-century. Whether you desire an intimate dinner or a large out-door wedding, the mansion's staff will attend to every detail with care.

You may experience the elegance of the Mansion personally by staying in one of the luxurious bed and breakfast suites. Relax in the parlor, antique-filled library, billiard room and sun-porch. A delightful five course breakfast awaits you after a restful night's sleep.

Victorian High Teas are served to the public by reservation and private teas are easily arranged. The tea is served by staff dressed in period clothes. Chadwick, the theatrical English butler, entertains you with piano playing prior to the tea. A tour of the Mansion and a short history talk follow the tea. The cost of this special event is $25 plus applicable taxes.

Secluded from the street, the beautifully landscaped grounds include lush lawns and gardens, a rose garden, a private gazebo and an ornate pergola. A carriage house and an enclosed secret garden round out the estate. Twenty-four years of meticulous private restoration have resulted in national recognition for this historic home. Your event, such as a private tea, could not be held in a more luxurious setting.

Cash/V/MC
Not Wheelchair Accessible
On-site Parking
Limited Street Parking

Tea is by reservation only.

Proprietors
Autograph_____Date_____

Elizabeth & Alexander's

English Tea Room
23808 Bothell-Everett Highway
Bothell, Washington 98021
425-489-9210
tearoom@e-a-englishtearoom.com
www.e-a-englishtearoom.com

From I-405, take exit # 26 and go toward Bothell on the Bothell-Everett Hwy (State Rt. 527). Go one mile and they are on the highway on the right side of the street next to Country Village.

Dean and Sue Hale built this tea room in 1998 and fashioned it after their son-in-law Alexander's Eastborne, England home town tea room. Each of the three warm and friendly rooms offers a unique ambience. The Parlor seats 20-25 and boasts an inviting fireplace. The Churchill Room, which accommodates 15-20, has s hunting theme and is decorated with bookcases and wingback chairs. Finally, the Alexander Room offers an intimate atmosphere with its capacity of only 5 to 10 guests.

Once settled in, you select your tea from the variety offered under the Barnes and Watson label. The tea sets begin with the Full Afternoon Tea which includes a scone, crumpet, jam, lemon curd and whipped cream, lemon tea cake, lemon tartlet, shortbreads, chocolate raspberry rum torte, fresh fruit and tea sandwiches-chicken salad, cucumber and cream cheese and smoked salmon. Other teas are Elizabeth's Tea offering a small scone with trimmings, fresh fruit, tea cookies, lemon/lime curd tartlet and lemon tea cake; and Alexander's Tea has assorted tea sandwiches, fresh fruit, crumpet w/lemon curd and shortbreads. A pot of tea is included in all of the above teas. The Children's Tea, for those under 12 years of age includes sandwiches, fresh fruit, shortbreads and a pot of hot chocolate. Dietary needs will be accommodated with advance notice and groups are welcome.

There are numerous breakfast items to choose from including quiche, Belgian waffles and maple pecan oatmeal. Some of the lunch items are Windsor Torte, chicken cashew salad and Ploughman's Lunch.

MC/V/DEB/Checks
Wheelchair Accessible
Lot Parking

Open Monday through Friday 9-3 (last tea 2:30) and Saturday 8-4 (last tea 3:30). They serve breakfast, lunch and afternoon tea. Tea time is from 11 to 3. Group reservations suggested 2 weeks in advance. Saturday reservations required 1 month in advance.

Proprietors
Autograph_____Date_____

Everything Tea

1015 First Street
Snohomish, Washington 98290
360-568-2267
everythingtea1@hotmail.com
www.everythingtea.net

From I-5 take Rt. 2 east to Bickford exit (first exit after Tresse/Historic Downtown). Bickford only goes south and changes into D Street. Continue until you get to First Street, turn left. They are on the south side of the street between A and B Streets.

Chris and Patricia call their business, Everything Tea, "1200 square feet of Tea Lover's Paradise." How right they are! There are over 270 loose teas and tisanes available in this shop, as well as a very large selection of tea accessories.

The shop is chock full of the "fun stuff" ... tea pots, kettles, cups and saucers, cozies and lots of unusual and handy accessories (those Drip Catchers really do prevent the spout from leaking!).

There are far too many tea labels to list but some examples are Bewley's, McGrath's, Ahmad, Barry's, Rishi Teas, Market Spice, Metropolitan Tea Co., and India Tea Co. Their house blend is Duncan's Ultimate Herbal Blend. As you can see, every kind of tea is represented and free tea sampling is available on Saturday and Sunday.

On one side of the room there is a cozy alcove with couches and tables, where you may take time for a little conversation, or you may choose to pick up one of the magazines on the "tea" table and get in a little reading while you sip.

Whatever your reason for visiting Snohomish, be sure to take time to check out this very friendly business, and catch up on the newest trends in teas.

MC/V/Cash
Wheelchair Accessible
Free Street Parking

The shop is open 7 days a week, Monday through Saturday 10-6 and Sunday 10-5.

Proprietors
Autograph_____Date_____

The Exhibitors Mall & Trellis Café

10312 - 120th Street E. # 4
Puyallup, Washington 98374
253-841-0769
kimariejohnson@yahoo.com
www.exhibitorsmall.com

Take Hwy 512 to Eatonville exit. Follow Meridian to 120th Street E., turn left, go one block. The building is on the right-hand side of the street.

Established in 1993, The Exhibitors Mall and Trellis Café offers delectable lunch fare in a cozy corner of the 5000 square food gift shop. Known for the best soups on Puyallup's South Hill, the café serves lunch 11 to 3 Monday through Thursday. Reservations are suggested for enjoying the optimal Tea experience. You will be served an assortment of finger sandwiches, scones, petit fours, seasonal fruit, a cup of delicious soup and endless tea. Enjoying tea in The Trellis Café can be compared to sitting in your favorite aunt's kitchen - warm, friendly and relaxed! Tea is $15.95 per person for adults and $13.95 for children. Want just a cup of tea and some of Fran's homemade bread pudding? No problem! When you are finished, you are invited to browse in the gift shop featuring local artists and major gift, home décor and retail lines. The dining room is available for private parties for young and old alike.

MC/V/Checks
Wheelchair Accessible
Lot Parking

The café serves lunch from 11 to 3 Monday through Thursday. Reservations are suggested for the tea set.

Proprietors
Autograph_____Date_____

Fairmont Olympic Hotel

411 University Street
Seattle, Washington 98101
206-621-1700 extension 3169
olympic@fairmont.com
www.fairmont.com/Seattle

From the south, as you near downtown, get into the left lane and take exit 165 (Seneca Street). From the light, go straight 2 blocks and move into the right lane. Turn right on 4th Street and go one block to University Street. Turn right and the hotel is on your right.

The luxurious Fairmont Olympic opened its doors in 1924, and has been considered Seattle's premier luxury hotel ever since. Boasting impeccable service, splendid Italian Renaissance architecture and two award-winning restaurants, the Olympic, listed on the National Register of Historic Places and a member of Historic Hotels of America, well deserves its reputation as Seattle's Grand Dame Hotel. This and additional information is available on their website.

An elegant Georgian Afternoon Tea is offered for $35 for adults and $18 for children, plus tax and gratuity. An example of the delicious tea sandwiches are - citrus prawn salad on rosemary bread, tarragon and almond chicken salad on eight grain bread, smoked salmon and Dungeness crab salad on white pin wheels, chicken/bacon/potato salad on wheat bread and cucumber & heirloom tomato Roquefort mousse on French country bread. Some of the luscious desserts are - a strawberry Bavarian tart, almond Tosca, apricot spritz cookie and coconut lamington.

The featured scone is a chucker cherry with Devonshire cream and raspberry jam. Your tea is selected from a list of loose-leaf teas which includes such traditional flavors as English Breakfast and Earl Grey to Japan Sencha and Kea Lani Orange Pineapple.

MC/V/AE/DIS
Wheelchair Accessible
Valet Parking-$19 for 2-3 hours
Hotel Lot-$14 for 2 to 3 hours
Limited Metered Street Parking

Tea is offered daily 11:30-2:30. Reservations are recommended.

Proprietors
Autograph_____Date_____

Fireside Room at the Sorrento Hotel

900 Madison Street
Seattle, Washington 98104
206-622-6400
charlie.evans@hotelsorrento.com
www.hotelsorrento.com

North on I-5, take Madison Street exit. They are on the corner of Madison and Terry. South on I-5, take James Street exit, go left on James and right on Terry.

Tea at The Sorrento is served in the Beautiful Fireside Room, where you are surrounded by opulence reminiscent of the early 20th century. The Fireside Room is very traditional for afternoon tea. Honduran mahogany walls add to rich fabrics and plush surroundings. Charlie Evans, the Hunt Club manager, calls the ambience "modern posh."

Reservations are required for Afternoon Tea and you may even reserve the day you plan to attend. Tea is only offered during the holidays during the months of November and December.

Afternoon Tea includes your choice of Numi Tea, and a selection of sweets and savories which may include salmon roulades, chicken curry barquettes, celery root salad in cucumber cups, fresh fruit tartlets, madelines, mini cream puffs, petít fours, chocolate pralines, miniature cookies and fresh baked apricot and cherry scones with Devonshire cream and preserves, for $35 per person. With any luck, you will be fortunate enough to take this exceptional tea by the 19th century Rookwood fireplace in one of the overstuffed leather chairs.

The Hunt Club, which adjoins the Fireside Room, is a full-service restaurant. Perhaps you will return for a stay at the Sorrento and a chance to try their other culinary creations.

MC/V/AE/DEB
Wheelchair Accessible
On-Street Parking. some are Metered
Parking Lot-$7 Validated Parking

Proprietors
Autograph_____Date_____

Foxwood House

125 Foxwood Drive
Newport, Washington 99156
509-447-2346
rjshawgo@povn.com

Foxwood House is on Hwy 2 between mile markers 328 and 329. They are a 35 minute drive north of Spokane. Watch for the billboard at Foxwood Drive.

When you see Foxwood House B and B, it is hard to believe that the owners, Roger and Jeanine Shawgo, did ninety percent of building it themselves. This modern day "Victorian" is absolutely beautiful, and the attention to detail amazing. Though only 7 years old, it looks like a home from the turn of the century. The furnishings are original items from the 1880s. They started offering afternoon tea to the public in 2004, and how lucky we are!

The dining room where tea is served is stunning. It boasts elegant antiques, and reproduction wall paper from the 1880s. Vintage Lenox Rose china, finger bowls at each place setting, 3-tiered servers, vintage linens, and ribbon bedecked dining chairs complete the elegant décor. For a really special touch, Roger and Jeanine dress in original clothing from the late 1880s and early 1900s while they serve you with great attention to detail.

A sample tea menu would include a first course of tea and scones with Devonshire cream, lemon curd and preserves. This is followed by three varieties of tea sandwiches which are served with fruit. Then comes a portion of raspberry sorbet. A second flavor of tea arrives with a 3-tier tray of desserts - usually cake, lemon tart, mini cheesecake, fruit cookie, chocolate-covered strawberry and a truffle. This generous menu changes weekly.

Special theme teas are offered throughout the year and the cost is $25. Janine sets the menu based on the occasion. Special dietary needs can be accommodated whenever making a reservation.

Cash/Checks
Not Wheelchair Accessible
On Site Parking

Tea is offered by reservation any day of the week. There is a required 3-4 day advance notice with a 24-hour cancellation policy. There is an 8-person minimum and 30-person maximum.

Proprietors
Autograph_____Date_____

Hattie's Restaurant

51 Cowlitz Street West
Castle Rock, Washington 98611
360-274-7019
hatties@hatties-castlerock.com
www.hatties-castlerock.com

From I-5, take exit 48 west into town on Huntington Avenue (approx. 1½ miles). At Cowlitz Street turn left, travel 2 blocks and you will see the restaurant on the left-hand side of the street, across from True Value.

Hattie's is gaining a reputation as a fun and interesting place to visit, whether for tea time, breakfast, lunch or dinner. The owner, Linda, offers what she calls, "Uptown class, down-home cooking," and that is precisely what you will find!

The atmosphere of the restaurant, ice cream parlor, Garden Room (complete with back porch and clothes line!), and Victorian "house" afford you the opportunity to choose your setting. The Victorian House, which is off the main dining room, boasts deep purple wall paper, period furniture, touches of lace, and décor that represents the Victorian era. This is a very special room set aside especially for tea. The main dining room is delightful and is the setting for a small re-creation of a country kitchen and parlor, complete with a fireplace. Hard to describe but delightful to see! As the name seems to imply, hats are everywhere, so if you feel a little under-dressed you may be tempted to don one of them, just as the servers do.

The breakfast menu is extensive and now features Linda's 'national award winning' Almond Stuffed Orange Glazed French Toast! For lunch you may choose from soup, salad, deli sandwiches, wraps, stuffed pitas, fish and chips, burgers or a custom-made baked potato. The signature chicken salad is one of the favorite offerings, whether served on a bed of lettuce or in a sandwich. Reservations are recommended for dinner and, again, the menu is extensive. If you plan to reserve for a group, Hattie's boasts the largest table in the Northwest at 16 feet 3 inches. It is a sight to behold!

Should tea time be your meal of choice, a special menu is prepared just for you. It consists of a scone, salad, a selection of small sandwiches, fruit, vegetables, cheese and sweets, plus a fragrant pot of tea, for $12.95 per person. This is just what I am looking for when seeking out the event called tea time!

MC/V/AE/DC/DIS/Checks
Wheelchair Accessible
Free Lot and Street Parking

Tea is by reservation only with a 48-hour notice required. There is a 24-hour cancellation policy. The restaurant hours are Monday through Saturday 8-8. Closed Sundays and most holidays.

Proprietors
Autograph_____Date_____

Hawthorn Tea Room

2208 N. 30th Street #101
Tacoma, Washington 98403
253-238-9021
teafriends@questoffice.net
www.thehawthorntearoom.com

From I-5 take exit 133 (City Center). Follow signs for I-705/Schuster Parkway. Travel along the waterfront. Follow sign for N. 30th Street/Old Town. The tearoom is on the left side of the street after the 1ˢᵗ traffic light at McCarver Street.

Casual elegance is how the owners, Laurie and Cathy, describe their tearoom. The walls are a sunny yellow and the floors are a custom treated material. The tables are decked out in linen cloths and fresh flowers to complete the welcoming ambience. A semi-private Victorian dining room is available for groups of up to 16 guests.

There are four tea sets to choose from, as well as a special one for children. The first tea is the Flutterby Cream Tea with two scones and fruit for $8. This is followed by the Light Luncheon Tea which offers a scone, fruit and tea sandwich for $10, and the Hawthorne Luncheon Tea which has a scone, fruit, assorted tea sandwiches and assorted sweets for $15. Finally there is the Monarch High Tea - soup, scone, fruit, assorted savories and/or tea sandwiches, and assorted sweets for $22 per person. All teas include a pot of tea and Devonshire cream, lemon curd and/or jam for your scones. The Children's Tea, for those 5-10 years old, is priced at $11 and it includes a scone with Devonshire cream and jam, fruit, choice of tea sandwich, cookies and tea, hot chocolate or lemonade.

There is a lunch menu that offers soup, sandwiches, salads, sweets and a selection of beverages. Boxed lunches, priced at $10, can be ordered on-site as well as by phone or fax.

A selection of loose teas and gift items are available for purchase.

MC/V/Cash
Wheelchair accessible
Free Street Parking

Open Tuesday-Saturday 10-4. Tea time is 10-3 with the last seating at 3. Special event teas are held throughout the year, i.e.; Spring, Mother's Day, Fall and Christmas. There is a $10 no-show fee for guests of large parties. Large groups of 17-32 can be accommodated on Sunday with prior arrangements. Groups of 2-16 can be accommodated Tuesday-Saturday. Reservations are recommended and two days notice required for special dietary needs.

Proprietors
Autograph_____Date_____

Healing Garden Tea Room & Flowers

111 N. Tacoma Avenue
Tacoma, Washington 98403
253-274-0861

From I-5, take the City Center exit, move right and follow directions for Schuster Parkway (705 N.). Get to the right and take Stadium Way exit. Turn right on Stadium Way, follow the road as it curves to N. 1st and N. Tacoma Avenue. Drive past the high school and turn right. They are 4 doors down.

This tea room opened in 2003 under the ownership of Fannie Kelley and it offers just the ambience "tea people" are looking for. Fannie calls her tea room an elegant, peaceful and quiet setting, and she invites you "to enjoy a beautiful tea experience with her."

The tea room features lavender and sage-green walls, floor-length sage-green tablecloths, floral top cloths and plants and greenery throughout. A second floor room is available for large groups or special functions. Special functions require a 30-day notice.

The afternoon tea menu has three tea sets to choose from. The Crème Tea of scones, fruit and nuts is $7; The Traditional Light Afternoon Tea includes a scone, fruit cup, nuts and dessert for $11; and the Healing Garden Light Afternoon Tea offers a scone, assorted savories, fruit cup and nuts for $16. The Full Afternoon Tea consists of a scone, assorted savories, fruit cup, nuts and assorted desserts for $22. Assorted savories are tea sandwiches, crackers with spreads and mini quiche. All teas include a pot of tea and lemon curd, preserves, creamed honey and Devonshire cream for the scones. The tea selection is extensive and it includes Republic of Tea, Ahmad Tea of London, Taylors of Harrogate and Market Spice.

Lunch items are on the à la carte menu and include sandwiches such as chicken salad, smoked salmon and cream cheese, and honey baked ham, priced from $6 to $7.50. Soups and salads are available for $2 to $4.50, and desserts are priced at $2.50 and $4.50. Beverages other than hot tea are also available.

Fannie's gift shop carries tea related items and silk flowers. Her tea shop adjoins the Custom Framing Company and Gallery.

MC/V/AE/DEB/DIS/Checks
Wheelchair Accessible
Street Parking

Hours are Wednesday through Saturday 11-6. The last tea service is 4:45. Anytime is tea time! Reservations are recommended for groups of 6 or more.

Proprietors
Autograph_____Date_____

La Connor Flats-A Garden

15920 Best Road
Mount Vernon, Washington 98273
360-466-3190
jen@laconnerflats.com
www.laconnerflats.com

From I-5, take exit 230. Follow Weston Hwy 20 for 5 miles to Best Road. Turn left on Best Road and go 2 miles. La Connor Flats will be on the right hand side of the road.

A short drive in the country brings you to this very special place. This oasis in the country is really beautiful and the hostess, Marjorie, most gracious. It must have surprised her to find two strangers knocking on her door in the late afternoon inquiring about her tea room. Actually, her tea room is a "retired" granary that has been converted into a charming and cheerful room … perfect for tea. Refinished hardwood floors and rustic barn board walls greet you, along with matching oak chairs and tables, set with double white linens and fresh flowers. The room, rich with light and a feeling of the outdoors, overlooks the beautiful garden.

The set tea is served on Depression glass, and Marjorie has over 200 cups and saucers in her collection and she uses these for her teas. The tea, which is served in three courses, consists of a fruit cup, hot scones and jam, a trio of sandwiches and assorted desserts for $12 plus gratuity. Other items may be substituted upon request. She also offers a Low Tea which includes a fresh fruit cup, tea and a fresh-baked scone with butter and homemade jam during festival days.

In the summer months, tea is served outside on the porch or in the beautiful English Country Garden. At one end of the garden there is a large gazebo which is used extensively for weddings and other celebrations. The gardens are open and in bloom, March through October, and the carpet of color is always changing. We found it enchanting when we visited during the month of September.

Cash/Checks
Lot Parking

The granary is open during April and serves soup/sandwiches during the Tulip Festival. Tea is by reservation, preferably at 2, throughout the year. Small groups should give at least 24-hour notice, 8-10 people minimum.

Proprietors
Autograph_____Date_____

La Tea Da Teas

at the Bradley House Inn
61 Main Street
Cathlamet, Washington 98612
360-795-3030
bradleyhouse@centurytel.net
www.bradleyhousebb.com

Take I-5 to Long View and Long Beach to SR 4, which will bring you right into Cathlamet. From Astoria, cross the Astoria Bridge then turn right to SR 4 to Cathlamet. They are near the last ferry to Oregon!

It just seems natural to me that a bed and breakfast would offer afternoon tea in the same tradition as the grand old hotels. Many B and Bs are in turn-of-the-century or early 1900s homes, with vintage furnishings and collections of memorabilia from the past ... a fine setting for tea. Bradley House is just such a place. Built in 1907 as a gracious home of a lumber baron, this elegant home sits on a knoll overlooking the historic town of Cathlamet, Puget Island and the mighty Columbia River. Tea is served in the dining room with its expansive fireplace and large lace-covered windows with floral valances. Shades of rose and pink give the room a soft welcoming feeling.

Audrian offers a large selection of themed teas from holiday to special occasion and each is custom-made to suit your wishes. A sample menu for High Tea might include jicama, green onions, slivered onions and parmesan cheese on Hawaiian bread, English cucumber marinated in rice vinegar and sea salt on white bread with cream cheese, mini quiche, grain cracker with fresh brie and dried apricots, orange cranberry scones with lemon curd, raspberry jam and Devonshire cream. The selection of desserts could be any of the following: petit four, mini cheesecake cube, cream puff or white chocolate macaroon. A selection of teas is included. You can enjoy all of this for $16.99 plus tax and gratuity. The tea menu varies and special needs may be accommodated. A gift shop is available for browsing.

Checks Accepted
Not Wheelchair Accessible
Street and Lot Parking

High Tea is by reservation only, with a 24-hour advance request. There is a 72-hour cancellation policy. House Teas are offered at Christmas, Valentine's Day, Easter and Mother's Day.

Proprietors
Autograph_____Date_____

Madam Fifi's Tea Room & Bakery

740-238th Street S.E., Suite B
Bothell, Washington 98021
425-483-2005
madam.fifis@yahoo.com / http://madam.fifis.tripod.com

From I-405, take exit 26 and drive south for 1 mile. They are located inside Country Village.

Madame Fifi's, the former Peach Tree Tea Room, was purchased by Christine in 2008 and has taken on a whole new look. It is now a whimsical wonderland where boas drape the walls and brown and aqua striped wall paper is accompanied by aqua paint and chocolate brown linens. Tables are set with beautiful blue and white china, put richly against the brown linens. Vintage picture of flappers, belly dancers and fairies accent the mood along with vintage music from the 1920's through the 1950's. Madame Fifi is pictured alongside a collection of eye candy which is displayed on an overhead surround shelf, and you'll be sure to delight in the vintage costume jewelry and vintage accessories.

For tea, one may choose the Quick Luncheon Tea which has assorted baked pastries and a plate of 4 tea sandwiches - turkey with raspberry cream cheese, smoked salmon with cc & cucumber, crab salad and chicken curry for $12.95. The Vegetarian Tea for Two includes a garden salad, 2 salmon cc & cucumber sandwiches, 2 tomato & cheese sandwiches and an assortment of fresh baked pastries for $28.95. The Afternoon Harvest Tea for Two offers a cup of soup and 3 sandwiches - 2 turkey with raspberry cc and 1 salmon with cc & cucumber, as well as an assortment of fresh bake pastries for $28.95. The Afternoon Garden Tea for Two, priced at $26.95, includes a garden salad, smoked salmon cucumber, turkey with raspberry cc and chicken curry sandwiches and assorted baked pastries. Finally, one may select Madam Fifi's Grand Tea priced at $19.95 per person. It offers a cup of soup or garden salad, fresh seasonal fruit, tea sandwiches- smoked salmon cc & cucumber, chicken curry, crab salad and turkey with raspberry cream cheese, and a dessert selection of tarts, cookies and pastries. All teas include a pot of tea and scones served with lemon curd and Danish cream. For the younger set there is Penelope's Tea for Kids which has fresh fruit, PB and J sandwich and mini cookies and a beverage choice for $10.95. The Teas for Two have a per-person price as well. Dietary needs for allergies only will be accommodated.

MC/V/Checks, Wheelchair Accessible
Large Parking Lot

This tea room has recently been sold. Please check with the tearoom for updates.

Proprietors
Autograph_____Date_____

Myrtles Tea House & Herbery

112 South Main Avenue
Ridgefield, Washington 98642
360-887-9018
ewb1003@msn.com
www.myrtlesteahouse.com

From I-5 North take exit 14 (Ridgefield/Pioneer Street). Take a left back over the freeway (Pioneer Street). Follow Pioneer Street about 3 miles. At flashing red light, go left and Myrtles will be on your left. The Wildlife Refuge is nearby.

Elizabeth Brush, who opened her tearoom in 2006, has done herself proud. Her grandmother, for whom the tea room is named, must be smiling down with pride, too. The historic street-level building, with its crisp white paint, expansive front porch and abundance of greenery, is the perfect location for tea. Our first impression when we entered this lovely tea room was "this is Casa Blanca". Maybe it was the very tall windows banked with floor-length green drapes and the high ceilings with fans featuring large leaf-shaped blades. Or perhaps it was the wicker and rattan furniture which was set off with potted palms. The table décor is soft and inviting - satiny green floor-length table cloths, tucked at the corners, covered with large pink toppers. Desert Rose dishes blend perfectly with the décor colors and truly fit the theme of this lovely tea room.

Tea choices are numerous, starting with the Wee Sipper for Children for $8 up to The Miz Myrtle Tea for $13.50. The latter offers sorbet, soup, sandwiches, savories, fresh fruit, scones and assorted sweets. Lighter fare includes The Gentlemen's Tea for $12 and The De "Lite" Deloverly Tea, with fruit and sandwiches, for $9. The Wentworth Tea, which adds soup and a sweet to the previous tea, is $11 and finally The Priscilla Club Tea, which is tea and scones for $8. All of the tea sets include a pot of tea and prices include tax. For those with special needs, most dietary needs can be accommodated.

Before leaving, be sure to allow yourself time to browse the herbery and gift shop. Besides being a great looking room, there is an abundance of temptation.

MC/V/AE/DEB/ Checks
Wheelchair Accessible
Free Street Parking

Open Wednesday through Saturday from 11:30 to 3. The last tea service is 2. Holiday Teas are offered from Thanksgiving to New Year's. Reservations are recommended and there is a 24 hour cancellation policy. Groups up to 35 can be accommodated.

Proprietors
Autograph_____Date_____

The Perennial Tea Room

1910 Post Alley
Seattle, Washington 98101
206-448-4054
888-448-4054
tealadies@perennialtearoom.com
www.perennialtearoom.com

Take I-5 from the north or south. Follow downtown exits to Pike Place Market.

Finding the Perennial Tea Room, which opened in 1990, was easy! We just followed the sidewalk at Pike Place Market north to the end. We then saw the bright floral windsock and very colorful window boxes strategically placed on the historic brick building. Both were an indication of the friendly and welcoming atmosphere we were about to enter.

The owner, Sue, engaged us in conversation and shared with us the extensive selection of 100 bulk teas and tisanes which they retail. They carry their own Perennial Tea Room label as well as Seattle restaurant favorite, Barnes and Watts. Each day four teas from their unique selections are brewed up, and one can have it served hot or iced. The emphasis here is on tasting something you may never have tried before.

Four small tables are set out for your relaxation, two inside and two outside. Should you wish to have a treat to go along with your tea, packaged shortbreads, Eccles cakes and McVitties biscuits are available for purchase.

While there we took time to look at the eclectic collection of gift items which were neatly placed on the many shelves that occupied the tea room. I was particularly interested in the selection of tea-related books while my daughter Alicia was fascinated by the art deco tea pots and tea cups. The gift choices were interesting and unlimited.

I would recommend that you take a bit more time to explore Pikes Market, which is a veritable hub of activity, but be sure to take a break and have a cuppa at Perennial Tea Room. You will enjoy both the tea and the visit with the owners, Sue and Julee.

There is limited on-street parking as well as a pay-parking garage.
Customers receive validation with a $20 purchase.

MC/V/DIS/AE/DEB/Checks
Wheelchair Accessible
Street Parking

Open daily from 9:30 to 6.

Proprietors
Autograph_____Date_____

Queen Mary Tea Room

2912 N.E. 55th Street
Seattle, Washington 98105
206-527-2770 / 877-527-2770
queenmary@queenmarytearoom.com / www.queenmarytea.com

From I-5, take exit 169 (45th Street) toward the University of Washington. Pass U.W., cross the overpass and immediately follow the loop to the right at the bottom. Go 1/2 block, turn right on 25th. Proceed to 55th and turn right, then go about 4 blocks.

Established in 1988, Queen Mary's is an authentic English Tea Room serving breakfast, lunch and traditional formal afternoon tea. The founder, Mary, calls her tea room, "theatrical Victorian fantasy," with its dark wood "ivy topped" wainscoting, and floor-to-ceiling draperies in floral shades of deep green and burnt orange. Lace curtains and cream-colored table linens, as well as silver teapots with flowers, give the room its finishing touches.

Formal Afternoon Tea, priced at $25.99, starts with a trio of sorbets served in a champagne glass, with a finger of shortbread on the side. This is followed by a tiered server laden with a generous portion of savories. Seasonally changed, it may consist of a trio of sandwiches like chicken almond, fresh cucumber and mint, and smoked salmon with cream cheese. Also on the server are a miniature scone, crumpet, English muffin, thumbprint jam cookie, London sugar cookie, lemon curd tart, chocolate raspberry teacake and assorted fresh seasonal fruit. The tea includes homemade whipped cream, jam, marmalade and a pot of tea. For an additional $5, the Royal Afternoon Tea includes a Mimosa, Dir Royale, Magnolia or Royal de Framboise. Queen Mary herself would have been impressed! Dietary needs may be accommodated with prior notice. Seasonal and themed teas are offered during the year and groups are welcome.

Breakfasts, which range from $7.49 to $12.59, include Bangers 'n' mash or Smoked Salmon Quiche. The lunch menu, which is extensive, also offers a variety of English favorites priced from $6.99 to $13.79.

The house tea is Queen Mary label, and it is available for purchase in the gift area, along with many other special items. Be sure to allow yourself time to look around.

MC/V/Checks, Wheelchair Accessible
Street Parking

Open Wednesday through Sunday 9-4. Anytime is teatime! Reservations are strongly recommended. Access to on-line web reservations are available 7 days a week and 24 hours a day through the Queen Mary Tea website www.queenmarytea.com. There is a 24-hour cancellation policy. Seasonal and themed teas are offered during the year. Groups are welcome.

Proprietors
Autograph_____Date_____

Ruby Sue's Tea & Treasures

625 First Street
La Conner, Washington 98277
360-466-9948
cforb@galaxynet.com

From I-5, take exit 230 W. to La Conner-Whitney Road. Make the left, going south to La Conner, then make the right turn at the Roundabout. Follow Morris Road until it ends, making the left on First Street. The tea room is about two thirds of the way up the street on the left.

Formerly called Chocolates for Breakfast and located in Oak Harbor, Susan made the move to La Conner in 2008. The tea room is painted in soft earth tones of taupe and sage, and it is accented with a majestic view of an ivory covered stone wall which is seen through floor to ceiling windows. The seating is elegant, complete with bone china, linen napkins and tablecloths. There are hats from the 1920s to 1950s available for the guests who wish to add that touch of formality to their tea experience. Gifts are displayed on Victorian shelves and antique display cases. A plush sofa and two exquisite high backed chairs are available for small groups desiring Low Tea.

The teas are priced are $9.95 to $18.95 and include the following selections. First there is a traditional Cream Tea with lemon curd and home-made clotted cream. Then there is the Afternoon Tea which includes soup of the day followed by a selection of scones, tea sandwiches, savories and sweets. The savories include quiche or crab tart, while shortbread, petite fours, truffles, tarts and locally grown fruits dipped in chocolate are counted among the sweets. These are presented on a tiered server which is decorated to represent the seasons. Your tea experience is completed with a scoop of lemon-drop sorbet served in a depression-glass goblet. A separate, less formal seating area and specialized menu is available for "Princess Parties" for children. This is often hosted by Mrs. Potts or Tinkerbell!

The tea seating area is in the rear of a tea and a gift shop which offers over 70 types of loose leaf tea, as well as teas and specialty foods from the United Kingdom, tea accutrements and other lovely gifts.

MC/V/DEB/Cash
Wheelchair Accessible
Free Street Parking/Municipal Lot

The shop is open from Monday, Wednesday, Thursday and Friday 11-5, and Saturday. Sunday hours are 1-5. Tea times are 11:15 for the Cream Tea, 2 for the Afternoon Tea, or as arranged by private parties. Private parties are booked and paid for in advance. A 50% refund will be granted to parties that cancel at least 4 days in advance.

Proprietors
Autograph_____Date_____

The Secret Garden Tea Room

1171 Elm Street E.
Sumner, Washington 98390
425-746-4557
secretgardentearoom@msn.com / www.sgtea.com

From Hwy. 167, exit onto Hwy. 410 to Sumner. Take 1st Street exit (Traffic Ave). At the end of the off ramp, turn left onto Traffic Avenue. At the 2nd traffic light, turn right onto Main Street and at next stop light, turn left onto Wood Avenue. They are on the left just after the big curve in the road.

This wonderful tea room was originally located inside a mall in Bellevue, but in 2006 moved to a beautiful "Painted Lady" located in nearby Sumner. Though it is a little further to drive for those coming from the north, it is well worth your time to travel to this tea room and to browse in nearby Sumner.

The Victorian mansion was built in the 1890s and has beautiful wood work throughout. Elizabeth has selected the colors of celadon, pale gold and bits of burgundy for her decor, and the colors blend beautifully with the original wood. Large windows grace each room and sheer curtains, graced by period style curtains, filter the sun. Tables are set with pure white linens, shiny silver, assorted china, and clear goblets. The eclectic tables and chairs add to the charm of the 3 dining rooms and the quaint sun room.

There are many tea sets to choose from starting with the Camellia Cream Tea for $9.95. The next two sets are available after 2:30. For $11.95 the Violet Sweet Tea includes the dessert of your choice, and the Lavender Light Afternoon Tea offers tea sandwiches, fresh fruit, and petite sweets for $14.95. Other choices are the Larkspur Luncheon tea which has sorbet, tea sandwiches, savories and sweets for $21.95 and the Hollyhock Tea which offers a cup of soup, tea sandwiches, savories, orzo pea salad and sweets for $24.95. Finally, there is the Rose Tea Celebration, offered for $31.95, which is presented in courses and requires that the entire party select this tea set. The tea set consists of sparkling cider, cheese and fruit plate, miniature keepsake tea cup with sorbet, tea sandwiches, savories, sweets and individual celebration cake. All of the teas include scones with Devonshire cream, jam and lemon curd and a pot of tea. The hardest part is making your choice!

For those wishing for other fare, the tea room offers brunch and lunch including soup, salads, sandwiches on croissants and quiche. All are home-made in their kitchen.

MC/V/DEB/Checks
Wheelchair accessible/Lot Parking

The tea room is open Wednesday-Sunday from 10-4. The gift shop is open until 5 p.m. Groups from 11-40 require reservations, which are highly recommended for everyone. Walk ins will be seated on a space available basis. Mother's Day and Victorian Christmas teas during December are offered.

Proprietors
Autograph_____Date_____

Steeped In Comfort

11016 Gravelly Lake Drive S.W.
Lakewood, Washington 98499
253-582-1336
margiemae1130@msn.com
www.steepedincomfort.com

From I-5, take exit 124. Follow Gravelly Lake Drive to 111th. They are across the street from Clover Park High School on Gravelly Lake Drive S.W. and 111th Street, 1/2 mile from Lakewood Towne Center.

This warm and inviting tea room was opened in 2004 and is now under the ownership of Margie Todd and her daughter-in-law Heidi Todd, a trained pastry chef. They offer an experience in "taking tea" that will relax the mind, refresh the body and renew the spirit.

The interior, with its Victorian country style, is done in shades of pastel and cream. There are 12 tables which are adorned with hand sewn linens and cloth napkins to match. Throughout the two rooms there are white shelves and assorted racks laden with a large selection of gifts and "necessi-teas."

Tea offerings are numerous, starting with the Victorian Cream Tea which offers a fruit tart with pastry cream and 2 scones for $7.95. The Lady Grey's Afternoon Tea, which is $15.95, includes a fruit tart, assorted sandwiches, savories and 2 scones. The Queen's High Tea has a fruit tart, assorted sandwiches, savories, assorted desserts and 2 scones for $20.95. Finally one may choose the Royal High Tea, which is a special order and requires 48 hours notice. This tea offers a fruit tart, hot savories of crab cakes, quiche Lorraine, stuffed mushrooms, roast beef & Havarti cheese baked in pastry and mini-baked pot pies. Assorted desserts and 2 scones are also included. The cost of the Royal High Tea is $25.95. All of the teas include a pot of tea. There is an à la carte menu offering soup, sandwiches, quiche, desserts and scones. For children, there is Princess Maisie's Tea for $8.95, which can be served at the Princess Table.

Numerous tea labels as well as coffee are offered. Special needs can be accommodated with advance requests and catered orders to go are offered for pick-up. Special teas are offered for Valentines, Mother's Day, Thanksgiving and Christmas.

MC/V/DEB if MC or VISA logo is on card
Wheelchair Accessible
Lot Parking

Hours of operation are Tuesday through Saturday from 11-4. Tea time is 11-2:30. The last tea service is 2:30. Reservations are strongly recommended, especially on Saturday. Groups are welcome with a maximum of 36. Large groups need 1 month reservation. See website for details.

Proprietors
Autograph_____Date_____

Tamara's Tea Room

at the Painters Cottage

321 Wellington Street
Walla Walla, Washington 99362
509-525-3182 / Dinners 509-200-1166
intimatedinners@hotmail.com

Take the Wilber Street exit off Hwy 12 in Walla Walla and drive 2 blocks to Isaacs Street (1st stop light) and turn right. Stay in the right hand lane. Turn right at Wellington Street. Turn right between Arby's and the Rent-a-Center. They are the cottage on the left side of the road.

In 2004, Tamara Krieger opened her tea room and she is now a full-service tea room. The décor is very sassy Victorian and the rooms are filled with eye candy and surprises in every nook and cranny-Victorian clothing, bone china, pottery and more. The Babies Room is filled with treasures for little ones you will be introducing to tea.

There are many tea sets to choose from starting with The Cottage Tea, which is a dessert tea for $9.00. The Rest-A-While Tea offers soup, salad or ½ sandwich, scone and a sweet treat for $9.50. Next is the Wellington Tea which includes choice of fruit, soup or salad, a tea tray of quiche, scones, sweet bread and 3 sweet treats for $11.00. The Ploughman's Plate has soup, salad or fruit, a tray of ½ sandwich selections, scone and 3 desserts for $15.00. The High Tea includes sorbet, soup, salad or fruit, tea tray with 4 different tea sandwiches, 3 types of bread, including a scone, and up to 5 desserts. All teas are served with unlimited tea of the day. For the younger set, The Teddy and Me tea is offered for $9.50 and it includes sandwiches, grapes, cheese cutouts, a scone, sweet treats and drink.

A monthly High Tea is held on the 3rd weekend and reservations are required. It is not held on major holidays. This tea includes 4 finger sandwiches or savories, 3 types of breads or scones, sweet biscuit, coffee cake or muffin and 4-5 bite-sized desserts for $15. *The Chocolate Extravaganza* is held in October and reservations are required. With a private tea, the customers may choose the items they wish to have. The tea room offers sugar-free and vegetarian food to those who make prior arrangements.

They are a full-range catering company, run by Intimate Dinners, and the tea room is available for all types of events. Cheese Louise is right next door so Tamara offers cheese and wine on their menu. You may sample cheeses before selecting some to take home. Tamara says that 'Cheese Louise adds a taste of the world to your tea experience"!

Major Credit Cards/Checks
Wheelchair Accessible
Large Parking Lot

Hours are Monday, Tuesday, Thursday, Friday and Saturday 10:30-5:00 and Sunday 11:30-3:30. They are closed on Wednesday.

Proprietors
Autograph_____Date_____

104

Taste & See Ministries

Inside of Angelica's B & B

1321 W. 9th Avenue
Spokane, Washington 99204
509-714-0097
info@tasteandseeministries.com
www.TasteAndSeeMinistries.com

From I-190 take the Maple Street exit. Head south and take a left on 9th. They are located on the corner of 9th and Cedar.

A Victorian Bed and Breakfast is the new home of Thada Ziegler's wonderful tea room. Formerly located in her home, and know as Taste & See Tea Room, Thada has found the perfect venue for afternoon tea. The tea room is a non-profit business and is associated with an organization which helps women in transition. To learn more about Thada's ministry, go to the website listed at the top of the page.

There is a tea bar where tea and scones are offered all day. Reservations are not required so walk-ins are welcome.

Tea time does require reservations. It is a delicious and generous 4 course tea that is offered for $20 plus tax and gratuity. The tea includes their signature huckleberry scones, 4 tea sandwiches, an assortment of desserts and tea. John and I have had the opportunity to take tea with Thada and it was a wonderful experience.

We recommend you put this on your list of must-do tea rooms where you can treat yourself, and at the same time, help women from the community. After tea, browse the gift area for unique and useful gifts.

Visa/MC/Checks
Not Wheelchair Accessible
Street Parking

Open Wednesday through Saturday from 9 to 4. There are two seating's for afternoon tea. Reservations can be made for any number between 2 and 25 guests.

Proprietors
Autograph_____Date_____

Taste the Moment

Restaurant & Tea Room
8110-164th Avenue N.E.
Redmond, Washington 98052
425-556-9838
info@tastethemoment.com
www.tastethemoment.com

From Seattle, take Hwy 520 east, WA. 202 W. exit towards Woodinville. Turn left onto Redmond Way/WA. 202N. Turn right onto 164th Avenue N.E. They are located on the right-hand side of the street a couple of blocks down.

A spring break tea room tour in Washington brought this tea room right to us. We were driving around Redmond, trying not to get lost, when we just happened upon this little gem. The new owner, Toni Monroe, opened for business in December 2004 as a restaurant. You may now reserve for tea!

The building is quaint and the two rooms quite pretty. White dominates the color scheme with white walls, linens, dishes and window covers. Even the gas fireplace at the end of the room is white. The ambience is French formal with lovely gilt touches around the room. Windows line one wall and give the room a light and airy feeling.

Afternoon tea is served in the small side room with the decorated arched entry. Toni decorates the tables with seasonal touches and uses pretty tiered servers and china to make tea special. The Royal Tea has a hot entrée, savory salad, fresh fruit and an assortment of pastries for $37. The Victorian Tea offers a tiered tower with assorted tea sandwiches, scones with crème fraichê and jam, and petite pastries for $26. Finally, the Taste the Moment Tea includes a raspberry or chocolate crepe, selection of breads, scone with crème fraichê and seasonal fruit for $15.95. All teas include a pot of Metropolitan Tea. For children, a pot of tea or apple juice, peanut butter and honey sandwich, fresh fruit and scone with jam is offered for $10.

MC/AE/V/DIS
Wheelchair Accessible
Lot Parking

Open Wednesday through Sunday 11-4. High tea is offered from 11-4. Reservations are not required but are preferred. Call for information on dinners and special events.

Proprietors
Autograph_____Date_____

The Tea Cup

204 N. Tower Avenue
Centralia, Washington 98531
360-807-1717
kathisteacup@localaccess.com

Take exit 82 and go east to Tower. Make a left on Tower. Travel 2 blocks and the tea room is on the right side of the street. They are located across from Centralia Flowers and Old Centerville.

This tea room, which was opened in 2003, is in a really great location in the older part of Centralia, where it is surrounded by quaint shops and antique stores. After a few hours of checking out the neighborhood, just settle in for a delightful tea prepared by Kathy Rogers and her capable staff. The extensive selection of teas is located on shelves where you can sniff before choosing ... a fun way to make your decision. Labels include Republic of Tea, Simpson and Vail, Numi, Burnes and Watson, and Twining.

Tea is served at small tables in the main area behind a "white picket fence". With the floral tablecloths, swags and flower arrangements, the room has a garden feel to it. In the back of the store, there is a cheery English Garden Room for special occasions or group gatherings.

Once settled in, it is time to make your selections for the High Tea. You have a choice of sandwiches, soup, desserts and scone for $15. A 15% gratuity is added for parties of 4 or more. The sandwich choices include salmon loaf, egg salad, cream cheese cucumber, ham and cheese, turkey cranberry, pecan chicken and qpple raisin.

If lunch is your meal of choice, you may select from a number of specialty wraps, soup of the day, and organic green salads. The beverage menu offers a variety of teas, coffees, pop, juice and smoothies.

Allow time for browsing, as the gift selection is large and varied. All are displayed on interesting shelves, racks and other settings.

MC/V/DEB/Checks
Wheelchair Accessible
Free Street Parking

The tea room is open Monday through Saturday 10-5. Tea is offered by reservation with 24 hour notification. There is a cancellation policy. Groups are welcome.

Proprietors
Autograph_____Date_____

Tea Room at Port Gamble

32279 Rainier Avenue
Port Gamble, Washington 98364
360-297-4225
tearoom@centurytel.net
www.tearoomatportgamble.com

From downtown Seattle, take the Washington State Ferry Service to Bainbridge Island. Follow Hwy 305 through Poulsbo to Hwy 3. Turn right (north) and continue to Port Gamble. Turn left at Gamble Bay. The nearest cross street is Hwy 104.

Janis and Scott purchased an existing tea room in the Historic Seaside Township of Port Gamble, WA in 2006. They have done a remarkable job transforming what once was just a building into a warm and inviting Victorian environment and experience. Customers are greeted by friendly owners and staff, and ladies are encouraged to wear one of the many hats that welcome them just inside the front doors.

Janis immediately implemented Little Girl Victorian Dress-up Parties and they have been a huge success. Teenage Etiquette Parties and Ladies Mystery Tea Parties are also available. Check their website for other events including Evening celebrations.

The tea choices start with a Cream Tea for $6.75. This is followed by a Breakfast Tea which is offered at $20.95. It includes quiche Florentine, scone, fruit tarts and fruit cup with Whipped cream. The final offering is the Chocolate High Tea priced at $22.95. This tea offers a variety of tea sandwiches, scone, tea cookie and a "truffle" of your choice, plus a fresh fruit chocolate fondue. All of the above include Devon cream, lemon curd and strawberry preserves for your scone as well as a choice of tea or French press coffee (regular or decaf). A number of "a la carte" items are available including a sandwich plate, quiche, scones, fresh fruit fondue, fruit cup, tarts and tea cookies and they range in price from $3.50 to $8.25. The Tea Room also offers offsite catering with complete staff to cover your wedding reception, birthday party, reunion dinner, etc.

Janie lovingly hand makes all the truffles and fudge that are sold in the store and gift shop area so be sure to select some to take home for later enjoyment.

This is an excellent choice for a day trip destination, one you will not likely forget. You will want to make a return visit as soon as possible!

Wheelchair Accessible
Street Parking

Open daily, except major holidays, 9-5. Tea time is by appointment. Please call or email for reservations, at least the day before. Notice of cancellation is appreciated.

Proprietors
Autograph_____Date_____

Tea Time Garden

P.O. Box 34
North Lakewood, Washington 98259
360-652-8488
mail@teatimegarden.com
www.teatimegarden.com

Contact Bonnie to make arrangements to purchase tea.

Bonnie Rose describes her business as, "extraordinary loose teas blended with herbs and spices, fruit and flowers, for a naturally delicious brew." Her blending studio is a fully licensed kitchen facility-creating custom blends for her mail-order business as well as for wholesale trade. The studio is not open to the public.

Bonnie grew up in a British household where loose tea was part of every day life. Every time there was a joy, sorrow or achievement, tea marked the occasion. In her youth, she developed an interest in plants and began cultivating many tea "tisane" herbs and true tea-blends. Her first successful tea recipe was at age seven and she still sells that blend today!

After a friend suggested that she package and sell some of her teas, she worked out several recipes, created a brochure and started up her own company - Tea Time Garden!

Today, Bonnie goes by the unusual job description of Teaist-a tea artist or 'one who blends teas,' and she considers herself incredibly fortunate to be able to create and sell something that has been so long a part of her life and one of her greatest pleasures. She is also an avid spinner, having learned to spin in 2003. She calls spinning sheer joy, moving meditation, and a place for her to ultimately relax, and she says that sitting in her spectacular gardens, drinking a pot of fragrant loose tea while spinning is heaven on earth!

Bonnie sells an extensive line of teas including black, green, herbals and a children's blend. Also for sale are several brewing accessories. Her teas come from India, Sri Lanka, China, Japan, Formosa and Africa. The ingredients and directions are enclosed with every bag of tea. To place an order, or for more information on her products, visit the website or you can reach Bonnie by email or telephone.

MC/V/DEB
Pay pal/Checks

Hours of operation are 9-5 on Monday through Friday.

Proprietors
Autograph_____Date_____

109

The Teacup

2207 Queen Anne Avenue N.
Seattle, Washington 98109
206-283-5931 / 877-841-4890
teacup@seattleteacup.com
www.seattleteacup.com

*From I-5, take the Seattle Center exit and follow arterial around Lake Union,
under the underpass, and past the Space Needle. Go right on Denny then right on
1st Street. From the north, go past Key Arena. Turn left on Roy and go one block.
Turn right on Queen Anne. They're between Boston and McGrew Streets.*

Owned by Elisabeth Knottingham, The Teacup was opened in 1991 and offers over
150 different loose teas, each hand-chosen by the staff and sold by the pound. Tea may be
purchased by the cup or by the pot. They also offer an ever-changing menu of scones,
cookies, tea breads and other treats.

There are shelves laden with tea accessories of every kind and tea may be purchased
in bulk.

After a refreshing cup of tea and a sweet treat, a walk around this charming
neighborhood is in order.

Wheelchair Accessible
Street Parking

Open 10-6, seven days a week.

Proprietors
Autograph_____Date_____

Tiger Mountain Tea Co.

317 N.W. Gilman Boulevard Suite # 47
Issaquah, Washington 98027
425-391-5009 / 888-691-5009
info@tigermtteaco.com
www.tigermtteaco.com

Take I-90 to Exit 17 (Front Street). Then go south on Front Street and right on Gilman Boulevard (West). Take the first left onto Juniper Street, then the third driveway on the right. The tea shop is at the west end of the parking lot. They are in Gilman Village in buildings 46 and 47.

This charming building is Olde World style with a British Colonial theme and Asian tendency. The tearoom, owned by Wayne Spence, has an organic, relaxing feel. It boasts dark mahogany woods, leather and chenille sofas and wicker and bamboo accents. Wayne says that while they are a tea shop, they are really about quality life style. Tea is meant to be experienced and they extend that experience through their entire shop.

Two special teas are offered. The Full Tea includes tea sandwiches (salmon & dill cream cheese, tea smoked chicken salad and marinated cucumber with watercress & cream cheese), scones with clotted cream and preserves, savories, seasonal fruit plate and a "sweets" plate. Priced at $24, this tea also includes an 18oz. pot of tea per person with refill. The second tea is the Child's Tea which is offered for $15. This tea includes tea sandwiches, fruit bowl, scone, cookie and age appropriate beverage.

There are numerous other food offerings. The Brunch Special, which is available anytime before 4, includes quiche, scone, fresh fruit and an 18oz. pot of tea for $9.75. Lunch, which is offered until 4, includes numerous sandwich choices from $5 to $7.50. Soup may be purchased by the cup or by the bowl and salads come in two portions priced at $4 and $6.50. For those looking for a sweet treat, there is a selection of desserts priced from $.85 to $4.50. Of course, scones may be purchased a la carte for $1.75 each and may be accompanied by one of the numerous beverages on the menu.

Loose teas, which carry their label, may be purchased and there is a gift area for browsing.

MC/V/AE/EBB/Checks
Wheelchair Access
Lot Parking

Hours are Monday, Tuesday, Wednesday and Saturday from 10-6; Thursday and Friday 10-7 and Sunday 11-5. Anytime is tea time. The last tea service is one hour before closing. They accommodate groups of up to 6 people. Reservations are required and Full Tea requires 48 hour advance notice. 24 hours is required for cancellation or other changes.

Proprietors
Autograph_____Date_____

Tudor Inn

1108 South Oak Street
Port Angeles, Washington 98362
360-452-3138 / 866-286-2224
info@tudorinn.com
www.tudorinn.com

Tudor Inn is located in an established residential district on a bluff above the waterfront and historic downtown area. The inn is on the corner of 11th and Oak.

This beautiful three-story, half-timbered home was built in 1910 by an English gentleman, and the original woodwork and a fir stairwell still grace this comfortable inn. It has been tastefully restored to retain the rustic charm of the Tudor era, and is decorated with many fine antiques from Europe. The inn has been modernized to provide the comfort and ease of the present. It is now the home of Betsy Reed Schultz, who is also the tea hostess.

In the dining room, a large table with ladder-back chairs is set before a wall of windows which share a view of the porch and lovely front yard. A period chandelier hangs above the table, and crisp white linens, candles, china and silver set the tone for an elegant and memorable tea.

Adjacent to the dining room is the main parlor, which has a grand piano and wood-burning fireplace, and where additional tea guests may be seated.

The elaborate Light Tea is served in courses and includes assorted juices, fruit compote, crumpets and scones with cream and jam, tea sandwiches, delicate cakes, cookies and tea or coffee. The cost of this experience is $15.95 per person. You are invited to "dress up" in your favorite hat and gloves, but should you not bring them, Betsy has extras of both!

Major Credit Card or Checks
Wheelchair Accessible
Free Street Parking

This Bed and Breakfast is open year-round and serves tea by reservations made at least one week in advance. Tea time is 12-3, October 15 through May 15, with one tea party per day. A non-refundable deposit is required.

Proprietors
Autograph_____Date_____

Victorian Connection Gifts & Tea Room

108 Vista Way
Kennewick, Washington 99336
509-783-3618
viconn@clearwire.net
www.victorianconnectiongifts.com

Hwy 395 north from Umatilla and make a right turn on Vista Way. From the south take a left on Vista Way. Clearwater joins Vista Way. The nearest cross street is 395 and Clearwater.

Isolyn and Simon refer to their tea room as a sanctuary for your soul. It is an elegant retreat where you can reminisce with friends about bygone days or those not so bygone. They invite you to enjoy scrumptious food and to sip a great cup of tea and their mission is to "pamper each guest and make them feel relaxed and special."

Afternoon Tea, which is offered at $13.50 plus tax, consists of scones, with Devonshire cream from England, curd and preserves, 3 or 4 different tea sandwiches, savories, pastries and tea. They continually fill your tea pot with boiling water to keep the tea hot! Each guest is given a choice of fine Ashby's Tea flavors, and they have many to choose from, including decaffeinated and herbal infusions. If lighter fare is your desire, you may choose the Cream Tea for $6.50 or a Sweet Tea for $5.25. Dietary needs can be accommodated.

The gift shop, which encompasses 1800 square feet, carries a large line of Ashby's tea, as well as a variety of preserves and curds from England. They also carry fine china and crystal, lamps, linens and lace, framed artwork, collectibles and much more. If there is something you are looking for but do not see in the gift shop, Isolyn will be more than happy to track it down for you. The emphasis is on service at Victorian Tea Connection.

MV/V/AE/Checks
Credit cards accepted if reserved by phone
Not Wheelchair Accessible
Lot Parking

Hours of operation are 10-6, Monday through Saturday. Tea time is 2-5 p.m. Reservations are required with a 1 day notice per person. No refund will be offered if reservation is cancelled. Maximum for groups is 18 guests. Teas offered on Mother's Day and at Christmas.

Proprietors
Autograph_____Date_____

The Victorian Gift Parlour

& Tea Room
9418 - 116th Street East
Puyallup, Washington 98373
253-445-1568

Coming from the North on I-5, take the 512 exit. Heading east on 512, take the 94th Street exit by South Hill Mall. Go south on 94th (past Tacoma Boy's) to 116th Street (4 blocks). Tacoma Boy's is on the corner of 94th and Gateway Real Estate is on the other corner.

"Sky" describes the tea room, which opened in 1989, as "very Victorian." There is lace everywhere, including hanging from the ceiling! Two tea rooms await you - one decorated in lavender and gold and the other in red. The soft glow of lamps filters through the rooms, and as Sky says, "When you enter, the perfume of tea begins to work its soothing magic." The atmosphere is very hushed and the soft sounds of a harp add to the very relaxing and peaceful ambience.

Sky offers morning or afternoon tea in the elegance of an Era Past. The set tea includes a choice of tea, fresh baked buttermilk scones, open faced cucumber hors d'oeuvres, pineapple cheese muffins and triple fudge brownies. The scones are served with whipped butter, Devonshire cream, Marionberry jam and lemon curd. All of this is offered for $12.50 per person.

For your browsing and shopping pleasure, there is an extensive gift area which offers English teapots, heritage lace, natural healing creams & oils and many other tea related accoutrements. So, enjoy your tea and extend your visit with a stroll through the lovely gift shop.

MC/V/DEB/Checks
Wheelchairs might be accommodated
Large Parking Lot and Street Parking

Hours are Tuesday through Saturday 11-5. Tea time is 11:30-2 by reservation. The last service is at 2. Groups of 2-14 guests can be accommodated. Large parties need a two week advance reservation. There is a 4 day advance cancellation policy.

Proprietors
Autograph_____Date_____

Victorian Rose Tea Room

1130 Bethel Avenue
Port Orchard, Washington 98366
360-876-5695
info@victorianrosetearoom.com
www.springhousegifts.com

From SR16, take the Tremont exit. From the north, follow the exit. From the south, take a right. Go straight until you reach the stoplight at Bethel Road. Take a left and go straight, keeping to the left at the Y until you see Village Square, which is located across from the Post Office. The tea room is the pink and blue building on the left.

    Victorian Rose Tea Room is in a charming "Painted Lady" style shop complete with a turret dining room. The beautiful pink building is something to behold and hard to miss. The interior is equally impressive.

    High Tea is offered by reservation on any day, usually at 3. The prices do not include tax and gratuity and *pre-paid reservations are required.* High Tea is $9.95 and it includes scones with whipped butter and jams, select fruit or veggies with dip, specialty desserts and tea or coffee. The Victorian Rose High Tea menu offers all of the above plus petite quiche and assorted tea sandwiches for $13.95. If you are hosting a party and would like your guests to leave with a special memento, a Fancy Floral Tea Cup may be added for $8.

    The breakfast menu offers quiche, e ggs Benedict, crêpes, and other specialties for $5.95 to $8.95. Lunch items include salads, specialty sandwiches and soup priced from $3.95 to $9.95. Dinner is now offered and you can contact the tea room for details.

    A lovely gift shop, Springtime Dolls and Gifts, adjoins the tea room. It features many popular collectibles as well as tea pots and tea sets. Take time to browse for that something special for yourself or a special someone!

MC/V/DIS/Checks
Wheelchair Accessible
Lot Parking

The shop is open Monday through Saturday 9-7 and Sunday 9-3. Breakfast is served from 9-11 and lunch is served from 11-4. Tea and desserts are available daily. Special teas are offered throughout the year. Call for more information.

Proprietors
Autograph_____Date_____

Wild Sage

World Teas, Tonics & Herbs

924 Washington Street
Port Townsend, Washington 98368
360-379-1222
wildsage@olypen.com
www.wildsageteas.com

Just off the Main Street (Water Street) on Washington, next to the fountain.

The world of tea is waiting to be discovered in this cozy, unique tea house in downtown Port Townsend. Featuring a wide assortment of more that 100 teas from around the world, the staff at Wild Sage is often quoted as saying, "So many teas, so little time." Specializing in supreme, full-leaf teas, Wild Sage features organic green and white teas, exquisite high mountain oolongs, flowering teas, wonderful black teas and unique herbal infusions from all over the world. Teas available in bulk can be sampled and experienced by the cup (to-go), or by the teapot (in-house), so one can "try, before they buy." Wild sage also offers packaged teas in tins and teabags, unique tea wares, classic and colorful teapots, tea tins, infuser mugs and other tea gifts.

Wild Sage provides a "sanctuary of earthly delights" to nurture the body, mind and spirit. Knowledgeable staff encourages the experience and discovery of tea, its ancient culture, the life style, and tea's many health benefits. Wild Sage also creates their own delicious, 100% organic herbal infusion blends, exclusive to this tea house, and Port Townsend. In addition to its wonderful selection of fine teas, Wild Sage also specializes in herbal health tonics, which are based on the Chinese "art of longevity." World teas, elixir tonics and organic herbs are artfully blended into delicious concoctions and served for "relaxation or rejuvenation."

This creative teahouse provides a serene retreat from the busy world. To accompany our teas, tonics or herbs, Wild Sage offers delicious, local baked goods, chocolates and simple snacks. Many customers are drawn to the store simply by its natural, enticing aroma. So, the next time you are in Port Townsend, Washington's Victorian seaport, amble into Wild Sage teahouse and re-discover the wonderful world of teas, tonics and herbs that are waiting for you.

MC/V/Cash
Wheelchair Accessible
Street Parking

Store hours are Monday through Saturday, 10-5:30 and Sunday, 11-5:30. Anytime is tea time!

Proprietors
Autograph_____Date_____

Your Cup of Tea

Certified Tea Etiquette Consultant & Speaker

Marysville, Washington 98270
360-658-8887
sss@yourcupoftea.org
www.yourcupoftea.org

Location is determined at the time of booking.

Susan Springer, a trained and certified Tea Etiquette Consultant, is the founder and director of Your Cup of Tea, a company which provides an opportunity for men, women and young people to learn proper etiquette for enjoying tea in social or business situations. Ms. Springer has a Bachelor of Arts degree in home economics, is certified in family and consumer sciences, is a member of and certified in Foundations of Tea-Level I and II by the Specialty Tea Institute, and is a graduate of the Protocol School of Washington, D.C., the leader in etiquette and protocol services. She is also a published author with works in Tea A Magazine, Tea Time Gazette, Tea Bits, and a columnist on tea-related topics for The Country Register of Western Washington newspaper.

With a delightful sense of humor, Ms. Springer presents the proper and correct protocols for tea and etiquette, and makes each presentation fun as well as educational for corporate workshops, retreats, tea rooms, clubs, churches and private events. The presentations are suitable for all genders and ages and are customized to meet your specific needs, budget and time requirements.

Susan is a consultant and is available by appointment.

Proprietors
Autograph_____Date_____

Welcome
To
Northern
California

An Afternoon to Remember

Tea Parlor & Gifts

452 Main Street
Newcastle, California 95658
916-663-6358 / 877-832-2736
info@afternoontoremember.com
www.afternoontoremember.com

From Sacramento, take I-80 toward Reno. Take exit 115. Turn left, go over freeway. Stay on road, past post office on right. Curve around Post Office, turn right on Main. They are in the left side of the street next to Place Sierra Bank.

We had the pleasure of sharing a taxi with the owner, Amy Lawrence, when we were in Las Vegas for a Tea Expo in 2004. What a delight she was to talk to, and our ride was over way too soon! Her enthusiasm for tea time is definitely reflected in her tea room.

The décor is European, with two rooms - the parlor and the garden room. Amy calls her tea room, "an elegant retreat where you can reminisce with friends, enjoy homemade food and sip a great cup of tea." Their mission is to pamper each guest and make them feel relaxed and special, while educating them about tea.

There are three tea sets to choose from, starting with a Cream Tea for $6.95. This is followed by the Light Afternoon Tea which includes 2 scones, 3 tea sandwiches and 3 tea desserts. Finally, there is a Full Afternoon Tea with a slice of quiche, soup/salad, 2 scones, 3 tea sandwiches and 3 tea desserts. All include a pot of tea, Devonshire cream and lemon curd. A vegetarian tea is available with advance notice. Their house tea is Crème Brule and they offer it for sale in bulk, as well as over 100 other fine loose-leaf teas.

After tea, take time to browse the gift shop for that something special to take home.

MC/V/AE/DEB/DIS/Checks
Wheelchair accessible
On-street Parking

Lots of pictures on their web site!

The gift shop is open Tuesday-Saturday 9-5 and Sunday 11-4. Tea times are Wednesday-Saturday at 11, 1 and 3, and Sunday 12 and 2. Groups of up to 48 can be accommodated.

Proprietors
Autograph_____Date_____

Benbow Hotel

445 Lake Benbow Drive
Garberville, California 95542
707-923-2124
1-800-355-3301
benbow@benbowinn.com
www.benbowinn.com

From Hwy 101, take exit 636. The Hotel is 2 miles south of Garberville and is close to Avenue of the Giants and Redwood State Parks.

    The Historic Benbow Inn, with its distinctive Tudor architecture and beautiful setting, has intrigued travelers for almost 8 decades. The "Hotel Benbow" opened to the public in 1926 and soon became a popular destination for motoring tourists traveling up the newly-completed Redwood Highway. The Benbow family sold the hotel in 1962 and each of the four subsequent owners has added personal touches and improvements, while preserving as much of the original work as possible. The Inn was placed on the National Register of Historic Places in 1983. The Benbow Inn's current owners, who bought the property in 1994, purchased the adjacent Benbow Valley Resort which includes an RV Park and a 35-par 9 hole golf course. Guests can also enjoy a pool, Jacuzzi, pro shop and store while staying at The Benbow Hotel.

    Complimentary Afternoon Tea is a tradition which the hotel continues to offer. Warm scones and piping hot tea are served daily in the beautiful lobby where one is surrounded by antiques, paintings, vintage photos, needlepoint and objects d'art - the perfect setting for tea. The tea service is set on a linen draped table in the center of the room. Fine white china, a silver urn and shiny spoons top the table, along with a large tray laden with home-baked scones. A silver tray holds the butter, jam and cream required for the perfect scones! We felt privileged to have the opportunity to take a cuppa here and look forward to our next visit to this area. Be sure to take time to check out the gift shop; there are some real treasures there.

MC/V/AE/DIS/Checks
Not Wheelchair Accessible
Lot Parking

Tea is served daily from 3 to 4. A special Teddy Bear Tea is also offered. Contact the hotel for the dates.

Proprietors
Autograph_____Date_____

Camellia Tea Room

828-1st Street
Benicia, California 94510
707-746-5293
camelliatearoom@yahoo.com
www.camelliatearoom.com

They are located in the historic downtown area off the I-780 freeway. Call for directions.

Located on a bustling street in the historic downtown area of Benicia, this charming tea room, which opened in 1995, is a wonderful respite from the day's errands and shopping. The beautifully restored 1897 building is surrounded by interesting shops and businesses as well as art studios and antique shops.

The interior is beautiful with the very high ceilings covered in Bradbury& Bradbury Art Wallpapers, ivory linen table coverings and fresh flowers on each table. Lace curtains grace the expansive windows and bone china adorns the tea tables.

There are three teas to choose from, as well as a Child's Tea for the younger set which is priced at $9. The Cream Tea is offered at $8.00 and includes 2 scones with strawberry jam and Devon cream along with a tea of your choice. The next two teas are offered for $9 each. For the Savory Tea, you will enjoy an assortment of finger sandwiches served with a tea of your choice. The Sweet Tea is served with an assortment of sweets with a tea of your choice. Finally The Traditional Tea, which is $20 and is served on a tiered server, includes an assortment of small finger sandwiches, 2 scones with jam and Devon Cream, an assortment of sweets, and tea of your choice. This tea is designed to serve one and is available all day.

A large selection of gift items and tea accutrements is set about on the many shelves and tables in the room. You will probably find something for yourself as well! Take time to look around and take in the beauty of this wonderful tea room.

Handicapped Accessible
Street Parking

The shop is open Tuesday through Sunday from 11-4.

Proprietors
Autograph_____Date_____

122

The Captain's Cottage Tea Parlor

& Gift Shoppe
2548 San Pablo Avenue
Pinole, California 94564
510-724-1470
www.captainscottagetearoom.com

From Hwy 80E, exit Pinole Valley Road. Take a left onto Pinole Valley Road. At fork in road, take a soft right to stay on Pinole Valley Road. Take a right onto San Pablo Avenue. They are on the left in the 1st block. From Hwy 80W, exit Pinole Valley Road. Take a right onto Pinole Valley Road. Follow directions as above.

It is hard to miss this beautiful home with its striking turret, bold color and abundant windows with bright white trim. Opened in 1999, the home offers three rooms to choose from - The Captain's Room is decorated in a nautical décor and seats 24, the Music Room features a variety of instruments and seats 10, and the Parlour surrounds you with everything tea and seats 10 guests.

The Captain's Tea is generous and varied starting with the first course of warm scones and crumpets served with Devonshire cream, lemon curd and fruit preserves. This is followed by a seasonal savory, baby greens with Maple-Mustard Vinaigrette and an assortment of miniature tea sandwiches. Finally the third course brings a variety of bite-sized delectable desserts. The tea includes a bottomless pot of tea and is offered at $17 per person.

For children, the Royal Prince or Royal Princess Tea is available for $17. It is a three course tea served on their exclusive Palace Teaware. The set includes scones and crumpets with preserves, lemon curd & preserves, gourmet sandwiches (cream cheese with jam, egg salad and mini hamburger), and "Let Them Eat" cakes. Beverage choices for this tea are tea, hot chocolate or fruit juice. There is a 6 guest minimum for this tea and a tiara craft is available for an additional $2.00 per child.

After tea, enjoy a walk among the many shelves of tea necessities, gifts and items for the home.

Lot Parking

The tea room is open Wednesday through Sunday with seatings between 11 a.m. and 1 p.m. Reservations are required. A non-refundable deposit of $100 is required for groups of 6 or more.

Proprietors
Autograph_____Date_____

Englund's Bistro & Tea Room

2002 Salvio Street
Concord, California 94520
925-691-8327
pammbarnett @aol.com
www.englundsbistro.com

They are located on the block between Todos Santos Plaza and The Brenden Theater in the downtown area.

The owners moved their business, Englund's Tea Cottage, from Clayton to Concord in 2008 and now bring their passion for great food to Englund's Bistro. The décor in the new restaurant is contemporary and elegant with taupe walls set off by burgundy and black accents.

Their tea experience offers a quieter atmosphere, linen and china service, scented warm hand towels, and traditional tea fare served on lovely three-tiered stands. There are two tea sets to choose from starting with the Stratford Tea which is offered at $16.95. It is plated and has a teacup of soup, 4 finger sandwiches and warm scones with Devonshire cream and jam. The Royal Tea is priced at $19.95 w/o champagne and $24.95 with. It includes a teacup of soup, 4 finger sandwiches, savory hors d'oeuvres, warm scones with jam & Devon cream, petit fours and 2 sweets. Both teas include warm towel service and a personal pot of tea. For the youngsters a Wee Tea, priced at $13.95, is available. It offers child friendly finger sandwiches, veggies & ranch dip, scone, sweet treat and orange honey tea or lemonade.

Englund's is a full service restaurant which offers lunch daily starting at 11 a.m. Hot and cold sandwiches, salads, soup and combinations are available. Dinner is offered after 5 p.m. and includes such items as Chicken Oscar, Steak Marsala and Lamb Chops. Desserts choices range from carrot cake and cobbler to a warm chocolate fondue, all priced at $5.95. Of course, scones can be purchased alone for $3.95!

A brunch is offered on Sundays and such temptations as eggs Benedict, quiche, biscuits & gravy and 4 egg burritos are on the menu. Prices range from $6.95 to $9.95. Champagne cocktails may be added to the brunch for $7. Dietary needs can be accommodated with prior arrangements.

This is a restaurant that seems to have it all!

MC/V/DEB
Wheelchair Accessible
Lot and Street Parking

Hours of operation are Monday & Tuesday 11-4, Wednesday thru Friday11-9 and Saturday & Sunday 9-9. Any time is tea time! Reservations are required for groups of 10 or more.

Proprietors
Autograph_____Date_____

Keeping Still Mountain Tea Shop

312 Broad Street
Nevada City, California 95959-2411
530-265-2367
info@keepingstillmountain.com
www.keepingstillmountain.com

From I-80, take the Auburn Exit (Hwy 49) to Grass Valley. Take the Broad Street exit at Nevada City. Stay on Broad until you see the Nevada Theatre on your right. Turn left at N.Y. Hotel.

Jick Icasiano opened her tea establishment in 2004 in a most interesting venue, the New York Hotel. Since Nevada City is such an interesting walk-about town, stopping to take a cup of tea is the perfect respite.

This is an Asian-style tea shop with a tea room upstairs. They carry over 70 varieties of tea, as well as a wide variety of tea accessories for purchase. Their premium gold-label selections are rare, limited productions and high-quality grade teas which you might brew for special occasions and serve to important guests. You may also indulge yourself and loved ones to a pot of tea as a sign of appreciation.

A 32 oz. pot of tea may be purchased for $7 and a 16 oz. pot for $3.74. Other beverage choices are iced tea and sparkling juice.

Bulk teas from all over the world, tea wares, books and gifts are available in the ground-floor gift shop. Asian art and furnishings have been added to their sales floor. Teas may also be ordered on-line.

V/MC/Checks
Wheelchair Accessible
Metered Public Parking Lot

Winter hours are Tuesday through Saturday 11-5. They stay open later on Friday and Saturday nights. Tea is served during open hours. Call for other hours of operation.

Proprietors
Autograph_____Date_____

Lakeport English Inn

675 North Main Street
Lakeport, California 95453
707-263-4317
LakeportEnglishInn@mcHSI.com
www.lakeportenglishinn.com

From Hwy 29, turn east onto 11th Street. At Main Street, turn right. Lakeport
English Inn is four blocks down on the right side of the street.

How special it was for me to discover that Lake County has a proper English Tea
Room. I spent my youth waterskiing at Clearlake, and skied across the lake from Lucerne
to Lakeport many a time. John and I met in Lake County and I look forward to returning
to this place, which holds so many memories, for afternoon tea!

The Lakeport English Inn gives guests a glimpse of England in a tea room
reminiscent of The Hotel Ritz in London. Karen Mackey opened her business in 2003
and the tea room is located in her lovely Bed and Breakfast Inn. Victorian colors and
design set the ambience for tea. The tables are decorated in shades of burgundy and white
and are set with crisp linens, fresh flowers and beautiful china & silver.

The London Ritz Tea, which is available on weekends and by special appointment, is
a full afternoon tea. The offerings include a selection of traditional tea sandwiches,
freshly baked scones with delicious preserves and Devonshire cream, tarts of the day, a
lovely selection of fresh dessert baking and coffee or tea. The tea choices are Pear Green
Tea and Mad Hatter's Tea Party, which is a Ceylon & Indian black tea.

Reservations are required for tea and must be made 3 days in advance. The seating
capacity is 35 guests. There is a gift shop, and of course, an invitation to spend time at the
Inn when visiting Lake County.

MC/V/AE/DEB/DIS/JCB
Wheelchair Accessible
On Street Parking

The Inn is open "24-7" but tea is offered on Saturday and Sunday with seatings at 12 and
2:30. Groups of 10 or more may be accommodated at any time. Special holiday teas are
offered from November 12th to December 18th.

Proprietors
Autograph_____Date_____

Lisa's Tea Treasures

Tea Salon & Gift Parlour
1875 S. Bascom Avenue # 165
Campbell, California 95008
408-371-7377
www.lisasteatreasures.com

From I-80 (Hwy.17 from the south), take the Hamilton Ave. exit. Go east on Hamilton 2 blocks. Turn right on Bascom and go 2 blocks to Pruneyard. Turn right into the parking lot. They are in the Pruneyard Shopping Center.

Dale-Ann Johnson opened her tea room in the perfect location … nestled among the many shops at the Pruneyard. This allows shoppers to take a quiet respite from the busy retail rush to enjoy a great afternoon tea and a steaming cuppa! In operation since 1997, this tea room exudes hospitality. You are greeted at the door and led to your table where you will see linen-clothed tables laden with china and silver, and a small bell to ring for service. The shades of green, burgundy and mauve lend themselves to the comfortable Victorian ambience. There are three rooms that can accommodate ten to twenty-five guests.

The tea set choices are numerous starting with the Queen Victoria Cream Tea, which is only available Mon.-Fri. and is priced at $13.95. For $18.95 you may choose from Tea Time Trio (salad, soup and scone), Lord William's Promise (a selection of tea sandwiches and a mini sweet), or Mademoiselle's Creation (mixed greens with seasonal berries, feta cheese and toasted almonds in a strawberry vinaigrette and a scone). At $22.95 your choices are Summer Regatta (scone, tuna salad tea sandwiches, goat cheese with sundried tomato sandwiches, mini mushroom tarts and a dessert choice), Venetian's Romance (scone, goat cheese and sundried tomato sandwiches, pesto nut tea sandwiches, roasted garlic and cheese puffs, and a dessert choice) and My Ladies Respite (scone, assorted tea sandwiches, a petite savory and a dessert selection), Louis XIV's Favorite (scone, Parisian chicken croissant tea sandwich, Roquefort pecan tea sandwiches, brie en croute and a dessert selection) and finally The Duchess Delight (scone, two each of egg salad supreme and cucumber mint tea sandwiches, quiche of the day and dessert). All scones are served with Devonshire cream and preserves, and all teas include your choice of hot tea, iced tea, cocoa, milk or lemonade. Dietary needs will be accommodated with advance request.

MC/V/DIS/ Checks/Cash
Wheelchair Accessible
Lot Parking

The shop hours are Monday through Saturday 11-5:30 and Sunday12-5.Tea time is anytime on weekdays from 11-4, Saturday at 11, 1:30 and 4 and Sunday from 12-5. The last tea time is 4 except Sunday when it is 3.

Proprietors
Autograph_____Date_____

Lisa's Tea Treasures

1175 Merrill Street
Menlo Park, California 95025
650-322-5544
www.lisastea.com

From Hwy. 280, take Sand Hill Road south to El Camino. Turn left on El Camino to Oak Grove (one block past Santa Cruz Ave). Turn right on Oak Grove. Go 1 block to Merrill and turn right. They are on your immediate right. They are near the Menlo Park Cal-Train Station and C of Commerce.

Dale-Anne opened this tea room in 2003, and continues to offer the same wonderful service that one enjoys at the Campbell location. The look, however, is a bit different. The ambience is of the European style, offering high ceilings and large windows. Shades of butter yellow and sage green are set off with raspberry accents. Tables are set with white linen cloths and napkins, white china and shiny silver. The chairs are upholstered and quite comfortable. Three rooms can accommodate private parties for ten to twenty-five guests. In favorable weather, outside seating is available for those who prefer the great outdoors!

The tea sets are the same as those offered at the Campbell location, and there are many wonderful choices. *Please refer to the previous page for specific information.* Besides those choices, both locations offer a special treat for the younger set. The Court Jesters Surprise, for those 12 and under, includes choice of tea, cocoa or milk, peanut butter and jelly sandwiches, pigs-in-a-blanket, pizza bites and sweets. It is offered for $15.95. Numerous side dishes can be purchased but they are served with Tea Plates only. Desserts can be purchased for $6.95

Both locations have gift areas which offer lovely tea cups and saucers, teapots, tea accutrements and gift items. Take time to browse for yourself or a friend.

MC/V/DIS/Checks/Cash
Wheelchair Accessible
Street Parking/Some Metered

Hours of operation are Tuesday through Saturday 11-5 and Sunday 12-5. Tea times are Tuesday through Friday 11-4. Saturday seatings are 11, 1:30 and 4. Sunday seatings are 12 and 3.

Proprietors
Autograph_____Date_____

Lovejoy's Tea Room

1351 Church Street
San Francisco, California 94114
415-648-5895
www.lovejoystearoom.com

Take Lombard to Divisadero. Turn right and follow until Divisadero becomes Castro. Follow Castro to Clipper and make a left turn. Take Clipper to Church. They are located on the corner of Church and Clipper.

This interesting and fun tea room first opened in the early 1990s, moving to its current location in Noe Valley in 2000. It was originally an antique store that served a good cup of tea. The customers become more interested in the tea and scones, and the rest, as they say, is history.

Warmed by light from the windows and shades of pink, the tea room is a welcoming place. Muna Nash, co-owner with Gillian Britley, likens it to "your eccentric great aunt's living room, cozy and cluttered." The tables, chairs, linens and china are all mismatched, and the result is a place that the owners feel reflects the diversity of San Francisco. It blends together the traditions of tea service with an eclectic, quirky and playful spirit.

Tea services are numerous and begin with a Sweet Tea for $10.95 and a Cream Tea for $12.95. They are followed by a Light Tea of one sandwich, scone, fresh fruit and shortbread tea biscuit for $15.95 and the High Tea featuring two sandwiches, coleslaw, greens, scone, fruit and tea biscuit for $17.95. The High Tea may be purchased for two with the addition of two sandwiches, a scone and one tea selection for $34. The Queen's Tea includes two sandwiches, coleslaw, greens, scone, and crumpet with lemon curd, fresh fruit, a petit four and a shortbread tea biscuit for $24.95. For children the Wee Tea is $13.95 and has a sandwich, scone, fresh fruit and tea or hot chocolate. All teas include a pot of tea, and double Devon cream and preserves for the scones.

A gift shop is located across the street, so be sure to take time to browse.

MC/V
Limited Wheelchair Access
2-Hour Metered Street Parking

Open Wednesday through Sunday 11-6. The last seating is 4:30. Reservations are recommended, especially on weekends.

Proprietors
Autograph_____Date_____

Mistletoe & Roses

121 W. Main Street
Turlock, California 93580
209-632-2178
contact@mistletoeandroses.com
www.mistletoeandroses.com

From Hwy 99, take Central Turlock/Main Street exit. Stay on Main Street to Historic Downtown Turlock. Mistletoe and Roses is in the Main Street Plaza.

Sisters Carol and Elaine Weber had a dream of some day owning a unique gift cottage, followed by the idea of offering tea. They realized that dream when, in 1998, they opened Mistletoe and Roses in Atwater, California. Then in 2001, they opened at their present location in Turlock's Main Street Plaza.

You may sit and have lunch or take tea in the English Tea Garden which features a gazebo, dining room and outside courtyard. The tearoom has lovely print yellow wallpaper, lace-covered tables, eclectic chairs and tables, and large cottage windows. All add to the charm of this English cottage tea room.

The Afternoon Tea, which requires reservations, includes soup in a teacup, fruit medley, scones with curd and cream, tea sandwiches, cheese and fruit for $23 per person (includes tax and gratuity). For lighter fare, there is a Cottage Tea Sampler which has tea sandwiches, fruit, cheese, scone with cream and curd for $9. Luncheon items include croissant sandwiches, specialty salads and a fruit and cheese platter, or soup and salad combinations priced from $6-$8 each. Desserts, scones and soup may be purchased à la carte and there are a number of beverages to choose from. Special dietary needs can be accommodated with prior arrangements.

Remember to take time to check out the gift shop which offers home accessories, English tea items, garden items and a charming baby section.

MC/V/AE/DIS/Checks
Wheelchair Accessible
Street and Lot Parking

The gift cottage is open Monday through Saturday 10-5. The tea garden is open Monday through Saturday 11-3, with the Queen Anne Tea being offered by reservation at 2.

Proprietors
Autograph_____Date_____

Ms. Lynn's Tea

120 N. Eleventh Street
Montague, California 96064
530-459-3439
mslynn@mslynnstea.com
www.mslynnstea.com

From I-5 in Yreka, take Hwy 3 east 6 miles to Montague. Go left on 11th Street and you will see the tea room two blocks down on the left.

Sometimes we have the good fortune to find a tea room just by chance. Such is the case with Ms. Lynn's ... and what a find. The short drive from the freeway is a trip to another time and place. Situated in the historic district of Montague, Ms. Lynn's is a true step back in time. One can easily imagine horses tied up in front of the building ... no asphalt and no sidewalk! Once inside, the feel of yesteryear continues. Antiques, lace, fine china and other evidence of time gone by abound. The large room, which is divided into two areas, offers gifts galore as well as comfortable seating areas for tea. The interior space accommodates 27, and the outside patio can seat 20, weather permitting.

The owner, Charlynn Long, puts a great deal of thought into your afternoon tea experience, from the beautiful table settings to the flower laden tiered servers and pedestal plates. Tea choices are numerous starting with the Cream Tea which consists of fruit, scones & tea breads or The Savory Tea which offers fresh fruit or vegetables with an assortment of finger sandwiches and scones for $11.95 each. The Dessert Tea, which is offered for $7.95, has your choice of one of their specialty desserts or a petite assortment. Finally The Queens Tea features a 1st course Chef's Choice along with assorted sandwiches and savories, fresh fruit, scones and petite assortment of desserts for $20.95. Scones are served with lemon curd and cream. All teas include your choice of tea. There are over 150 loose teas to choose from including Rishi and their own house blends and all are available in bulk.

MC/V/AE/DEB/DIS/Checks
Wheelchair accessible
Street Parking

The tea room is open Wednesday from 10-4. Reservations are requested for tea. Cancel reservations within 24 hours if possible. Special theme or holiday teas are offered. Sunday brunch is available by reservation.

Proprietors
Autograph_____Date_____

Rose Mountain Manor Tea Room

233 Plutes Way
Colfax, California 95713
866-444-7673
innkeeper@rosemountainmanor.com
www.rosemountainmanor.com

Take I-80 12 miles past Auburn to the Canyon Way exit (just after Weimar). Turn left on Canyon Way and go about 6 miles. Pass Sierra Chevrolet, the Antique Mall and a brown building with red trim. Turn right on Old Illinoistown Road. Go 1/2 mile up the hill. There are 2 forks in the road with pink Rose Mountain Manor signs. At the first fork, go left and at the second go right. The manor is the first house on the left.

Rose Mountain Manor is situated on five wooded acres in the historic town of Colfax in the Sierra Foothills. The town is filled with charm and small town atmosphere, and is only 15 minutes from Auburn, Grass Valley and Nevada City. The house is a large yellow Victorian which boasts beautifully appointed rooms and outstanding hospitality.

Afternoon tea is offered at 4 each night to overnight guests. It consists of delicate homemade scones and tea breads. High Tea is offered Wednesday through Sunday from 11am-2pm at a cost of $19.95. It is available to the general public with 24 hour advance reservation. The three course tea includes finger sandwiches, quiche, a seasonal salad or soup, fruit, tea breads, scones and dessert. They also feature a children's menu.

The owner, Barbara Bowers, invites you to host your next bridal or birthday shower, birthday party, Red Hat event or women's group meeting at her gracious and cozy home.

There is a gift area that features china tea cups, teapots and tea accessories.

High tea is served Wednesday through Sunday 11 a.m.-2 p.m.

Proprietors
Autograph_____Date_____

Secret Garden Tea House

721 Lincoln Way
San Francisco, California 94122
415-566-8834
sgtea@comcast.net
www.secretgardenteahouse.net

Traveling south on 19th Avenue, turn right on Lincoln Way. Go 10 blocks and the tea room is on the left hand side of the street between 8th and 9th.

Following an afternoon of wandering through Golden Gate Park, what better way to relax than to take tea at this wonderful tea house. Just across from the park, Annie has created a warm and welcoming oasis. The décor offers intimate tables covered in pink floral cloths and white ladder-back chairs. White chandeliers, white shelves and matching rose floral china complete the charming ambience.

The numerous tea sets are served on white-plated tiered servers and include your choice of tea, cocoa, milk or lemonade. Scones are served with Double Devon Cream and preserves. For $10.95, the Lady's Cream Tea offers two scones. At $13.95 you may choose Oscar's Surprise which includes a scone, 2 mini pastries, short bread and fresh fruit or Sweet Surrender, which offers a selection of mini tea pastries, tea cakes, short bread and fresh fruit. The Garden Escape has a tasty selection of bite-sized snacks, savories and canapés for $14.95. Earl's Favorite includes 6 tea sandwiches, fruit, and a crumpet or muffin for $16.95. Finally, The Bedford's Delight has a scone, 6 assorted tea sandwiches, a savory and a selection of tea pastries or the dessert of the day for $19.95. The sandwich choices are: cucumber with light Bleu cheese and mint, chicken with toasted almonds, mango chutney and sharp English cheddar, curried egg with spring onion and fresh cilantro, ham, apricot and raisin, and smoked turkey with lemon caper cream and baby dill. For children twelve and under, there is a Prince or Princess tea which includes a peanut butter and jelly sandwich, a mini chocolate brownie, a pig in a blanket, delightful petit four and beverage for $14.95. Annie also offers teas for special occasions such as birthdays and showers. Light lunches are also available.

MC/V/AE/DIS/DEB
Wheelchair accessible
Enter Golden Gate Park at 9th Avenue and go right to park on
Martin Luther King Blvd.

Tea time is offered Tuesday through Friday 12-5. Saturday and Sunday seatings are at 11, 1:30 and 4. Reservations and pre-orders are recommended. The gift parlor is open noon to 5:30.

Proprietors
Autograph_____Date_____

Tea Garden Springs

38 Miller Avenue
Mill Valley, California 94941
415-389-7123
blanche@teagardenspring.com
www.teagardensprings.com

From Hwy101, take E. Blithedale/Tiburon exit. From north, take a left and from south, take a right. Continue straight through lights in residential-looking area. When you enter the "small town", go left on Sunnydale & park. They are above Jenni Lows Chinese Restaurant on the village square.

This beautiful Asian-themed teahouse, which is a tribute to the old days of China, is a special meeting place evoking ancient temples and natural springs. The décor is red, gold, green and neutrals and features plants, a stream and Buddha wall hangings. The longevity of the teahouse, opened in 1994, is a testament to its success.

You are invited to arrive early and sip a calming cup of tea or vitalizing herbal elixir in their serenely beautiful tea garden as you prepare to receive an experience of touch or you may choose to take tea after your treatment.

Tea Garden Springs is a holistic health spa, a Zen spa of vision, health and vitality. It is important to note that they do not replace medical services. Numerous spa body therapies are offered and each treatment ends with a Dosha-specific herbal tea elixir and chyawanprash, a rejuvenating health tonic.

You are offered specific Ayurvedic home care advice and products to incorporate into your life. Each week they offer an evening of group meditation followed by a discussion to help you enquire into present experience, rediscover what you already know and deepen your practice through meditation.

Numerous Chinese green teas and blended herbals, as well as teapots and tea sets are available for purchase. If you wish to just enjoy a cup of tea, it is available for purchase. Tea, which is served in wonderful yising tea pots, comes with an almond or sesame cookie.

Credit card and address are required at the time of booking. 24-hour cancellation notice is required or your reservation will be subject to a minimum charge of $60 for each hour of service booked.

MC/V/AE/DEB/JBC/DIS/Checks
Not Wheelchair Accessible
Lot and Metered Street Parking

The shop is open Monday 11-7, Tuesday through Saturday 9:30-7:30 and Sunday 12-7:30. All day is "Tea Time." Groups from 3-25 are welcome.

Proprietors
Autograph_____Date_____

Tea Time

542 Ramona Street
Palo Alto, California 94301
1-650-328-2877
contact@tea-time.com
www.tea-time.com

They are in downtown Palo Alto between University Avenue and Hamilton. The nearest landmark is City Hall.

Tea Time tea room is located in the heart of downtown Palo Alto and is situated northwest of the Silicon Valley and south of San Francisco. Visitors are told that they are in a beautiful spot that has the flair of a Southern European city and the convenience of the American way of life.

On Ramona Street, Tea Time is located next to many restaurants, bars and art galleries. It is the only tea room in the area that offers fine teas from around the world and here people can buy their teas from over 120 choices. The loose leaf tea is then professionally packed in a bag or tin according to your preference.

In the Spring of 2006 the lounge went through a total make-over. The seating area now has 32 seats with nice bamboo designed tables and chairs. The counters have been upgraded with marble counter tops from Italy, and the solid oak shelves display for sale finely designed tea pots and cups & saucers in antique as well as contemporary designs. On the walls you can admire nice pictures of tea plantations from Asia, contemporary Asian art and painting s made by young and upcoming artists.

You can order your favorite fine tea in the tea lounge brewed on the spot. You can also enjoy traditional English tea sandwiches, crumpets, soup, salad and a wide assortment of desserts and English scones while listening to background music. Jazz and classical music contribute to the soothing atmosphere of the tea lounge. Thao invites you to experience it yourself!

MC/V/DEB/Checks
Wheelchair Accessible
On-Street Parking

Hours are Monday through Saturday from 10:30 until 7 and Sunday from 10:30 until 6. Any time is tea time!

Proprietors
Autograph_____Date_____

Teance / Celadon Fine Teas

1780 Fourth Street
Berkeley, California 94710
510-524-2832
info@teance.com
www.teance.com

Take Hwy 80 to the Albany exit, which is after Berkeley. The landmark Theater Albany is next door.

Winnie Yu calls Teance, which opened in 2002, "an oasis of calm aesthetic." The 1600 square foot shop is a skylight environment with sustainable bamboo cabinetry, raked plaster walls, and hand-made glazed porcelain tiles. The centerpiece, made of concrete, is a round tea bar which is used for tea tasting. Cheng Design of California, an award winning designer, created this oasis. Table service is available and it seats about 30 guests. A running waterfall fountain also acts as another bar.

Winnie tells us that they specialize in premium whole-leaf teas from China, Taiwan, Japan and Korea, and that their tea service is strictly Asian style. The teas are imported directly from farms. Education is very important to them and customers visit Teance to learn about teas at the tea bar.

The tea selections include ultra-low caffeine whites, hand-picked greens, no-caffeine florals & medicinals, a large selection of oolongs, and 100% oxidized red and black teas. There is also a selection of cold tea drinks.

Orders are per pot and there is a 10% discount for 2 orders shared in the same pot. Remember to ask your server for the pastry selection of the day.

If you wish to purchase one of these teas to enjoy at home, Teance sells them in bulk. They also offer beautiful, and some "one of a kind" tea wares for sale as well as a new line of tea-infused chocolates.

MC/V/Checks
Wheelchair Accessible
Lot and Street Parking

Business hours are Monday-Sunday 10 a.m.-7 p.m. Tea bar hours are Monday-Sunday 10 a.m.-6 p.m. The tea room is open Saturday and Sunday from 11 a.m. to 6 p.m. Store hours change from November 23rd to December 23rd.

Proprietors
Autograph_____Date_____

Treasured Tea Time

3214 Riverside Boulevard
Sacramento, California 95818
916-930-9401
treasuredteatime@netscape.net
www.treasuredteatime.com

I-80 west, exit at 10th Street. Go left on Riverside Boulevard (about 1 mile). They are on the left side of the street across from Vic's Ice Cream. I-5/99N, exit Sutterville Road to right. Continue veering right until Riverside. Go right on Riverside (about 1/2 mile), they are on the right side of the street.

As you enter the tea room, which was opened by Cheryl and Larry Steuck in 2001, you are first struck by the bright-yellow walls in this Victorian themed venue. White Battenberg lace-covered shelves hold a wonderful selection of gifts and tea accoutrements. Small round glass-topped white tables are covered with Battenberg lace cloths, white linen napkins, and antique silver pieces - cream and sugar, tongs, silverware and demitasse spoons. Soft candle light on each table is the final touch promoting calm & conversation.

Before being served, you select a tea cup and saucer from Cheryl's collection of over 100. Gold mirrors and candle chandeliers grace a corner of the room where you can choose the perfect hat, drape and gloves.

The Tea Time presentation features 3-tiered trays laden with home-made scones (2 per person), lemon curd and Devonshire cream, finger sandwiches, fresh fruit & cheeses, teatime tarts, cookies and breads. Hot or cold soup is served with individual 2-cup pots of tea of your choice. Fresh roses adorn each tiered tray for that final touch of elegance. The menu changes monthly on the first Saturday.

Cheryl has also been catering since 1998 and can accommodate up to 350 guests. She requires a $300 minimum per event.

Treasured Teatime carries a selection of 80 teas which may be purchased in bulk in the extensive gift area. Allow yourself time to look around!

MC/V/DIS/AE/DEB
Wheelchair Accessible
Lot Parking

The shop is open Tuesday through Saturday 10-6 and Sunday 1-5. Tea service is available Tuesday through Friday 12 and 2 p.m., Saturday 11, 1 and 3, and Sunday at 2 p.m. Reservations are recommended, especially Thursday through Sunday. Cancellations less than 24 hours in advance will be charged 1/2 the cost.

Proprietors
Autograph_____Date_____

Tyme for Tea & Co.

37501 Niles Boulevard
Fremont, California 94536
510-790-0944
www.tymefortea.com

From I-880 take the Alvarado Niles exit and head east. Alvarado Niles turns into Niles Boulevard. The tearoom is on the corner of Niles and H Streets.

Thyme for Tea was opened in 1996 in a building that is over 100 years old ... the perfect ambience for afternoon tea. Owned by Jessica Rodriquez, it is located in the historic Niles District of Fremont. Inside the tearoom the tables are covered in pink cloths and are adorned with fresh flowers and an assortment of beautiful tea cups. You will dine among beautiful antiques and collectibles, for what Jessica describes as "an enchanting tea experience."

The tea offerings are numerous and begin with Tea and Tea Pastries which includes assorted decadent pastries and seasonal fruit, or Tea and Tea Sandwiches, offering 5 tea sandwiches, seasonal fruit and assorted pastries, each for $14. This is followed by the Victorian Tea which is a three course tea that includes a scone, 5 assorted tea sandwiches and 3 tea pastries for $21. Finally, you may choose the 3 course Grand Sparkling Victorian Tea. It offers a scone, a glass of champagne, 5 assorted tea sandwiches and 3 tea pastries for $24. All of the tea sets include your choice of tea. Scones are served with Crème Fraiche, lemon curd and raspberry preserves.

If you wish something other than a tea set, there are luncheon choices. You may select a chicken pecan croissant sandwich or Waldorf albacore tuna salad sandwich, both of which include fresh fruit, for $13. Seasonal soup or salad is also available for $9. Just want dessert? There is a daily special for $5!

This tea room features many items perfect for browsing while awaiting your appointed tea time or following your tea experience. Antiques and collectibles are set about the store and include antique furniture, jewelry, tea pots and accessories, garden items, fountains, vintage clothing and more.

MC/V/AE/DEB/DIS/JCB/Checks
Wheelchair Accessible
Street and City Parking Lot

Open daily from 11am to 5pm. Tea room hours are Monday through Friday noon to 3pm. Saturday and Sunday tea room hours are 11 a.m. to 4 p.m. Jessica offers Christmas and Holiday Teas featuring harpist Kathryn Honey, Halloween Brew Ball, Valentines Cupid's Touch and a Mother's Day Tea.

Proprietors
Autograph_____Date_____

Vasquez House

414 E. First Street
Sonoma, California 95476
707-938-0510
www.sonomaleague.org/vasquez.html

Take Hwy 101 to Hwy 37 exit Sonoma. Follow signs to Sonoma and you will enter Sonoma on Broadway. Stay on Broadway to the Plaza. Turn right then left and the building is in a courtyard in the center of the block. It is located between E. Napa and E. Spain Streets in an area called El Paseo.

The historic Vasquez house was built in the early 1850's for General "Fighting Joe" Hooker of Civil War fame. He sold the house and adjoining land to Catherine Vasquez and her husband, Pedro. The family occupied the home until 1901. In 1974 the house was donated to the Sonoma League for Historic Preservation and it was moved to its present location in El Paseo de Sonoma.

Reconstruction of the dwelling was undertaken by members of the League with donations of materials and labor from local residents and businessmen. The downstairs portion of the house has been converted into a library and an attractive Tea Shop, done up in the period of the house.

Though not a full service tea room, this charming house is a great place to get away from the hustle and bustle of the busy street. The room is small but can accommodate 11 in the winter and 20 in the summer. We were there during the summer on a very hot day, and enjoyed a generous glass of iced tea, though hot tea was an option. Be sure to allow yourself to indulge in one of the delicious sweets that are also available - pie, cookies or cake! If tea is not your beverage of choice, coffee and lemonade are also on the menu.

I recommend that you include a stop at Vasquez House for tea when you are spending the day in historic Sonoma.

Checks/Cash
Wheelchair Accessible
On Street Parking

The home is open to the public from 2-4:30, Thursday through Saturday. Tea may be purchased until 4. Special groups can reserve a month in advance.

Proprietors
Autograph_____Date_____

Windsor Tea Room

at the King George Hotel
334 Mason Street
San Francisco, California 94102
415-781-5050 ext. 158
800-288-6005
foodbev@kinggeorge.com

The hotel is located 7 blocks from Union Square on Mason Street between Geary and O'Farrell Streets.

Whenever I go "home" I seek out a tea room to visit. This was a destination for us some years ago, and we found it to have a very warm and welcoming English ambience. The beautiful burgundy carpet, with its gold crown pattern, is set off by the white linen-covered tables, and centerpieces chosen to suit the occasion. You are surrounded by royal works of art, and are treated to classical music playing in the background. The location of the Windsor Tea Room is one of San Francisco's many classic boutique hotels, and it is close to the core of the city. You may easily reach it by bus or cab, or for the more ambitious it is walking distance from Union Square and the cable car line.

The King George Tea has a scone with fresh whipped cream and preserves, a selection of tea sandwiches, a variety of petite desserts, and a bottomless pot of Lindsey's Tea. It is offered for $24.95. The Royal High Tea includes all of the above as well as Champagne or sparkling apple cider for $29.95. The sandwich selection includes salmon, ham & cheese, egg salad, cucumber and chicken salad.

For children under 10, the Teddy Bear Tea has a choice of tea, chocolate milk or hot chocolate, a scone with cream and preserves, a PB& J sandwich, Nutella sandwich, petit fours and chocolate truffle. This tea also comes with a 5-inch plush teddy and it is offered for $15.95.

The holiday teas, which have varied prices, include a complete tea plus some special surprises!

MC/V/AE/DEB/DIS/JCB
Wheelchair Accessible
Lot Parking

Tea is by reservation and is served from Thanksgiving to New Years, as well as at Easter and Mother's Day. Groups of 10 or more can arrange a private tea with prior arrangements.

Proprietors
Autograph_____Date_____

Welcome

to

Favorite

Recipes

Beverages

Christmas Tree Tea

"A la Fontaine"
Albany, Oregon

1 Douglas Fir Tree

Take the tips of a Douglas fir tree and snip into pieces (from the stem up to 1/4" diameter). Steep in boiling hot water 30 minutes. Sweeten to taste. It is rich in Vitamin C.

This recipe was used by Native Americans and is wonderful at Christmas. It is also very refreshing chilled in the summer.

Printed with permission.

Iced Green Tea

"The Tea and Herb Shop"
Corvallis, Oregon

4 Tbsp. Dazhang Mountain Green Tea
1 Tbsp. peppermint leaves
1 Tbsp. lemon balm
1 tsp. fresh grated ginger
Pinch of lavender flowers

Bring 4 cups of water to a boil. Put ingredients in boiling water and stir. Steep for 5 minutes and strain. Add 3 1/2 cups cold water. Refrigerate until cold, then serve over ice.

Mint Tea Punch

"Some of our Favorites"
The Bountiful Beauties and Colorful Cuties
Red Hat Chapter-Vancouver, Washington

8 tea bags
8 fresh mint sprigs
1 cup sugar
2 qts. boiling water
2 1/2 cups pineapple juice
1 can (6 oz.) frozen lemonade concentrate, thawed
Additional mint sprigs for garnish

Combine tea bags, sugar and mint sprigs. Pour boiling water over tea mixture. Cover and let steep for at least a half hour. Remove and discard tea bags and mint sprigs. Transfer to a large pitcher or punch bowl. Add pineapple juice and lemonade concentrate (undiluted). Stir well; serve over ice garnished with mint sprigs.

Makes 3 quarts

My Favorite Chai

"Taking Time for Tea"
Diana Rosen

1 1/2 cups water
8 green cardamom pods, crushed
6 whole black peppercorns
2 slices fresh gingerroot, peeled and diced
1 stick cinnamon, 2 inches long
2 whole cloves
2/3 cups whole or soy milk
4 tsp. sugar
3 tsp. loose-leaf black Assam tea

Warm two teacups by filling them with hot water and covering them with their saucers. Set aside.

In a saucepan, bring the water and spices to the boil. Reduce heat to low and simmer for about 6 minutes.

Add the milk and sugar, and heat to almost boiling. Add the tea leaves and turn off the heat. Let the tea infuse for 3 minutes, or longer, to taste.

Strain into cups and serve.

Red Rose Tea

"The Book of Afternoon Tea"
Lesley Mackley

3 Tbsp. Ceylon breakfast tea, or to taste
4 1/4 cups lukewarm water
Sugar, to taste
Few drops of rosewater, to taste
12 ice cubes
6 mint sprigs
Fresh rose petals

Put tea in a bowl. Pour warm water over tea and let stand overnight.

Strain tea into a large pitcher. Stir in sugar and rosewater, and then add ice cubes. Place a mint sprig and a few rose petals in each of 6 glasses. Pour tea on top.

Makes 6 servings

Variations: For Vanilla Iced Tea, omit rosewater. Instead, put a vanilla bean in the bowl with tea and soak overnight. Remove before serving.

For Mint tea, omit the rosewater and rose petals. Put a mint sprig in bowl with tea to soak overnight. Remove it before serving. Garnish with mint sprig.

Victorian Iced Tea

"Foxwood House"
Newport, Washington

4 individual tea bags
4 cups boiling water
1 can (11 1/2 oz.) frozen cranberry-raspberry
juice concentrate, thawed
4 cups cold water

Place tea bags in a teapot, add boiling water. Cover and steep for 5 minutes. Remove and discard tea bags. Refrigerate tea in a covered container. Just before serving, combine cranberry-raspberry concentrate and cold water in a 2 1/2 quart pitcher, stir in tea.

Serve over ice. Garnish with mint.

Yield: 10-1 cup servings

Sandwiches

Savories

Salads

Soups

Bacon Cheese Potato Soup

Rose Mountain Manor
Colfax, California

1 large onion, chopped
½ cup chopped green pepper
6 pieces chopped crisp bacon
2 Tbsp. butter
4 medium potatoes, peeled and sliced
4 cups chicken broth or bouillon
2 cups milk
10 oz. Velveeta cheese
Black pepper to taste
Chopped parsley

Sauté first 2 ingredients in butter in saucepan. Add bacon, potatoes and broth. Bring to a boil, reduce heat and cover. Simmer 15 minutes or until potatoes are tender. Stir in milk, cheese and pepper. Cook over low heat until cheese is melted and soup is hot, stirring occasionally. Sprinkle with parsley.

Serves 6

Bacon Cheddar Tease

"Ms. Lynn's Tea Table"
Carol Perlick

8 oz, cheddar cheese (finely shredded)
1/2 cup mayonnaise
3 Tbsp. onion (finely chopped)
1/2 cup real bacon bits
Triscuit Thin Crisps

Mix all ingredients except crackers until well blended. Place crackers on cookie sheet. Top each cracker with about 1 tsp. cheese mixture. Broil 2 minutes or until cheese is melted. Garnish with chopped red and green pepper, if desired.

Reprinted with permission.

Bacon Tomato Sandwiches

"Tea Cozy Cooking"
Diane Lareau AmEnde

16 oz. cream cheese, softened
1 cup (1 medium) chopped & seeded tomato, drained
8 slices bacon, cooked crisp and chopped
1 Tbsp. dried basil leaves
Pumpernickel bread

Place ingredients, except bread, in food processor and thoroughly combine. Chill spread for at least 2 hours before first use so that flavors develop. Allow to come to room temperature before using.

Spread filling on one slice of bread. Cover with second slice of bread. Remove crusts and cut into 4 pieces. Serve immediately or place on holding plate and cover with damp paper towel and plastic wrap and chill until serving time.

Yield: 6-8 servings

Broccoli and Cranberry Salad

"Ms. Lynn's Tea Table and More"
Carole Perlick

4 cups cut up broccoli
1/4 cup sunflower seeds
1/2 cup chopped red onion
3/4 cup cooked bacon
1/2 cup dried cranberries

Dressing

1 cup mayonnaise
2 Tbsp. rice vinegar or red wine vinegar
1/4 cup sugar

Mix all ingredients for the salad. Broccoli may be used fresh or partially cooked.

Whisk dressing ingredients together, and then pour over the salad. Keep refrigerated until serving.

Cheddar Cheese Wafers

"A Year of teas at the Elmwood Inn"
Shelley and Bruce Richardson

2 cups sharp cheddar cheese, softened
2 cups self-raising flour
2 cups crispy rice cereal
2 sticks butter, softened
1 tsp. salt
1/2 tsp. red pepper

Mix all ingredients by hand in a large bowl. Roll into small balls. Place on an ungreased cookie sheet and flatten each with a fork. Bake at 350° for ten minutes.

Makes 3 dozen

Reprinted with permission.

Cherry Salad

"Some of Our Favorites"
The Bountiful Beauties and Colorful Cuties
Red Hat Chapter-Vancouver, Washington

1 can cherry pie filling
1 can pineapple (chunks or tidbits) drained
1 can Eagle Brand condensed milk
1/2 cup pecans or walnuts
1 med. Size Cool Whip

Mix the first 4 ingredients then fold in the Cool Whip. Chill at least one hour before serving.

Reprinted with permission
Contact TeaRoomsNorthwest@hotmail.com for
information regarding purchasing this cookbook

Chicken Waldorf Tea Sandwiches

"Lisa's Tea Treaures"
Menlo Park, California

3 red delicious apples
4 cups chopped chicken
1/4 cup lemon curd
1 tsp. lemon juice
1/2 tsp. cinnamon
1/4 cup raisins
1 cup mayonnaise
3/4 to 1 cup sour cream

Peel and chop apples and mix with lemon juice. Mix apples, with chicken, mayonnaise, lemon curd and sour cream until blended. Add spices, nuts, raisins and stir (add more sour cream if needed for spreading consistency). Refrigerate 4-6 hours or overnight. Spread filling on bread and top with second piece of bread. Trim crusts and cut into quarters (triangles, squares or fingers). Dip one edge in chopped toasted walnuts, if desired.

Chicken with Dill Tea Sandwiches

"An Afternoon to Remember"
Newcastle, California

2 cups chicken
1/2 pkg. Italian dressing
1/2 cup loosely packed fresh dill, chopped
2 Tbsp. snipped chive
Salt and pepper to taste
mayonnaise
Dried parsley for garnish
Butter
6 slices buttermilk bread

Lightly pulse chicken in food processor or chop finely. Mix all ingredients Add just enough mayonnaise to bind the mixture together. Spread butter on bread. Add filling and top with second slice. Cut into desired shapes. Sprinkle dried parsley on sides of sandwiches for garnish if desired.

Makes 12 tea sandwiches
(3 big sandwiches cut into 4 pieces)

Chilled Apricot Citrus Soup

"Pomeroy House"
Yacolt, Washington

2-12 oz. apricot nectar
1/4 to 1/2 cups sugar
2 Tbsp. corn starch
2 Tbsp. water
1 Tbsp. lemon juice
2 Tbsp. lime juice
1/2 cup orange juice

In a medium saucepan, bring nectar to a boil then add sugar. In a measuring cup, blend cornstarch and water. Add to juice mixture and bring to a boil, stirring constantly. Stir in lemon, lime and orange juices.

Serve cold.

Cream of Carrot Soup

"Althea's Tea Room"
Dallas, Oregon

3/4 cups chopped onions
1 qt. chicken stock
2 Tbsp. uncooked white rice
2 Tbsp. butter
3 cups chopped carrots
2 tsp. tomato paste
Salt and white pepper to taste
1/2 cup heavy cream

Cook onions slowly in butter for about 5 minutes, until soft but not brown. Add stock, carrots, tomato paste, and rice. Simmer for 30 minutes or until carrots are fork tender. Puree in a blender or food processor. Return soup to a pan and add cream, stirring slowly. Season to taste. It can be reheated in a microwave. Store covered in the refrigerator.

Pat serves this soup every Wednesday.

Cucumber with
Mint Butter Sandwich

"Tea Time at the Inn"
Gail Greco

2 Tbsp. sour cream
1 oz. fresh mint leaves, chopped
4 sticks sweet butter
1/8 tsp. salt
3 to 4 large cucumbers, peeled and sliced thin
60 slices thin white bread

In food processor, blend sour cream and mint. Add butter. Blend well. Spread half the slices with a thin layer of the mint butter. Add 5 to 6 cucumber slices to each half, overlapping slices slightly. Add tops. Remove crusts. Cut sandwiches in half lengthwise.

Yield: 60 sandwiches

Curried Chicken Salad

"Leach Botanical Gardens"
Portland, Oregon

2 cups finely-chopped chicken
1/4 cup finely-chopped celery
1 small apple, peeled and grated
1 Tbsp. chives
1/3 cup mayonnaise
1 tsp. curry powder
1/4 tsp. salt
1/4 cup chopped peanuts (optional)

Combine first four ingredients. Mix mayonnaise with curry powder and salt then add to chicken mixture. Add peanuts if desired.

This mix can be used as a salad or for cream puffs or sandwiches. Makes about 2 1/2 cups, enough for 40 puffs or 8-10 sandwiches.

Feta Cheese Cups

"Breakfast at Ten, Tea at Four"
Sue Carroll

8 slices firm white bread
1/4 cup butter, melted (1/8 pound)
1 large egg, beaten
3 oz. softened cream cheese
3/4 cup crumbled feta cheese (3 oz)

Preheat the oven to 350°. Grease 24 miniature muffin cups. Using a 2-inch cookie cutter, cut the bread into rounds to fit the muffin cups. Brush one side of the bread with the melted butter and fit into the muffin cup buttered side down.

Combine the egg, cream cheese, and feta cheese. Drop 1 teaspoon of the cheese mixture into each muffin cup.

Bake for 20 minutes or until puffy and lightly browned.

Yield: 24 cheese cups

Fruit and Nut Tea Sandwich

"Hawthorn Tea Room"
Tacoma, Washington

1-8 oz. cream cheese
1 medium Granny Smith apple, diced
1 rib celery, diced
1/2 cup golden raisins
1/4 cup dried cranberries
1/4 cup dried apricots, chopped
1/4 cup cashews, chopped

Combine all ingredients, spread on hearty wheat bread. Enjoy!

Kiwi-Bleu Cheese Tea Sandwiches

"Lisa's Tea Treasures"
Campbell, California

Cream cheese
Sour cream
Bleu cheese

Combine equal parts of above ingredients. Blend well and stir in equal part of chopped, toasted pecans. Spread on dense white bread and cut into desired shapes. Top with twists of fresh kiwi.

Lavender Grilled Salmon or Steelhead

"Hood River lavender Farm"
Hood River. Oregon

3 lb. salmon fillet
4 Tbsp. honey
6 Tbsp. virgin olive oil
1 Tbsp. lavender, crushed
or run through a coffee grinder
1/4 cup white wine
1 Tbsp. Worcestershire sauce
1 Tbsp. lime or lemon juice

Place all ingredients, except salmon, in saucepan over moderate heat, stirring with a wire whisk at all times until ingredients are reduced by one-third, to create a sauce. When sauce has cooled slightly, brush on salmon.

Grill or bake salmon until flaky (don't overcook), about 10 minutes, basting with sauce. Set some sauce aside to pour on salmon before serving.

Printed with permission.
Contact-www.lavenderdaze.com
1800-LAV-FARM

Mammy's Country Ham & Tomato Tartlet

"The Tea Experience" from Teatime Magazine

Cream cheese pastry (recipe follows)
2 large eggs
1 cup half-and-half
1/2 tsp. salt
1/3 tsp. ground black pepper
3/4 cup grated Cheddar cheese
1/2 cup country ham, finely chopped
1/2 cup Roma tomatoes, finely chopped
1 Tbsp. finely chopped chive

Preheat oven to 350°. Lightly coat mini-muffin tins with cooking spray. On lightly floured surface, roll cream cheese pastry dough to 1/8" thickness. Using a 2" cutter, cut pastry. Place pastry rounds in well of prepared muffin tins. In a large bowl, whisk eggs, half and half, salt and pepper. Sprinkle cheese, ham and tomatoes in pastry shells. Cover with egg mixture and sprinkle with chives. Bake 40-45 minutes or until golden brown.

Cream Cheese Pastry

1 (3oz) cream cheese softened
1/2 cup margarine, softened
1 cup flour

In electric mixer combine cream cheese and butter; blend in flour. Shape into balls. Refrigerate 4-5 hours.

Mini Lobster Rolls

"Tea Party"
Tracy Stern with Christie Matheson

12 oz cooked shelled lobster meat, cut into
1/2" chunks
1/2 cup margarine
1/2 cup finely diced celery
1 Tbsp. minced fresh dill
Salt and white pepper
8 hot dog buns

Combine lobster, mayonnaise, celery and dill with salt and pepper to taste. Trim the ends from the hot dog buns and then cut each bun in half. Fill the buns and serve.

Makes 16 sandwiches

Mushroom Pasties

"The Secret Garden Tea Room"
Sumner, Washington

1 lb. mushrooms, trimmed and sliced 1 1/4 inch thick
1 tsp. pepper
1 Tbsp. Italian herbs
2 cloves garlic, minced very fine
1 tsp. salt
2oz. cream cheese, softened
1 pkg. frozen puff pastry sheets, thawed
1/4 cup parsley, chopped

Sauté mushrooms, pepper and herbs together in pan, cooking until most of the liquid is evaporated. Add salt and garlic just before removing from heat. Cool slightly, then place in food process or and add cream cheese. Pulse just to combine; do not puree mushrooms. Refrigerate until ready to make pasties.

To Assemble pasties: Cut puff pastry into 2 1/2 inch squares, then gently pat and stretch each square to make it 3x3 inches. Place 1 rounded teaspoon of mixture in center of each square, brush edges with water and fold in half diagonally to make a triangle. Press edges with the tines of a fork to seal. Brush top with cream, sprinkle with chopped parsley and bake at 400° for 12-15 minutes until light golden brown. Serve immediately, or store in refrigerator and reheat in 375° oven for about 5 minutes. They may be frozen and thawed in refrigerator before warming.

Sausage Rolls

"America's Best Tea Room Recipes"
Lady Caroline's British Tea Shop
Omaha, Nebraska

2 sheets flaky puff pastry
12 pork sausage links
Egg wash for glaze (egg mined with a bit of water)

Preheat oven to 350°. Cut sausage links apart, lay end to end, 1" from the side of 1 puff pastry sheet. Fold the edge of the puff pastry up and over the sausage. Cut long roll of sausage from pastry and press cut edge with a fork to enclose. Cut into 1" sections and place individual sausage rolls on a lightly greased baking sheet. Continue with remaining sausages and puff pastry. Glaze sausage rolls with egg wash. Bake for 25 minutes, until golden brown. Tip baking sheet to allow grease to run away from sausage rolls. Place rolls on paper towels to drain. Serve warm.

Reprinted with permission

Scotch Broth

"Teas Me"
Sherwood, Oregon

1 1/2 pounds of lean beef or mutton
3/4 cup pearl barley soaked for 12 hours in cold water
4 onions, sliced
2 cup diced carrots
2 cup diced turnips
1 cup peas
3 quarts boiling water
2 tsp. salt

Combine all ingredients except salt in a kettle. Cover with a tight fitting lid and simmer for 3 hours, stirring occasionally. Season before serving.

Serves 8

Shrimp with Dill Butter

"Celebrating Tea"
from Teatime Magazine

24 large fresh shrimp, steamed
12 slices country white bread
1/2 cup butter, softened
1 (3 oz) package cream cheese, softened
2 tsp. minced fresh dill
1/2 tsp. minced fresh chives
Garnish: fresh dill sprigs

Peel and devein shrimp. Using a 2" square cutter, cut each bread slice into 2 squares. In small bowl, combine butter, cream cheese, minced dill and chives. Spread thin layer of butter mixture over each bread square. Place one shrimp in center. Garnish with dill sprigs, if desired.

Makes 24 sandwiches

Smoked Salmon-Stuffed Endive

"Celebrating Tea"
from Teatime Magazine

1 (8 oz) package cream cheese, softened
1/4 cup sour cream
1 green onion, minced
1 (4 oz) package thinly sliced smoked salmon
1 (4 oz) package fresh alfalfa sprouts
16 Belgian endive leaves (about 2 heads)

In small bowl, combine cream cheese, sour cream and green onion. Cover and chill. Cut each slice of salmon into 4 equal pieces. Wrap salmon around a small bunch of sprouts. Place each salmon roll on endive leaf. Pipe or dollop cream cheese mixture evenly on each. Refrigerate until ready to serve.

Makes 16 endives

Strawberry-Spinach Salad

"Tea Cozy Cooking"
Diane Lareau AmEnde

10 oz. bag torn baby spinach
1 pint strawberries, cut into bite-sized pieces (make sure you choose ripe and juicy berries as they are the focal point of this salad)

Dressing

1/2 cup sugar
2 Tbsp. sesame seeds
1 Tbsp. poppy seeds
1 1/2 tsp. minced dried onions
1/4 tsp. Worcestershire sauce
1/4 tsp. paprika
1/2 cup canola oil
1/4 cup cider vinegar

In a blender or food processor, combine dressing ingredients. Blend well. Add a few drops of water if dressing is too thick. In a large bowl (or divide into small bowls) arrange spinach with strawberries on top. Drizzle dressing over salad and serve immediately. Chill any leftover dressing.

Yield: 4-6 servings

Stuffed Olive and Swiss Layered Tea Sandwich
"Cheryl's Treasured Tea Time"
Sacramento, California

2 slices brown pan bread
1 slice white bread
Softened cream cheese
2 slices Swiss cheese
Processed stuffed green olives
Baby chives

Spread soft cream cheese on 2 slices of brown bread, and butter both sides of the single slice of white bread. Add a slice of Swiss cheese on top of each slice of brown bread. Spread mixture of green olives on each slice of cheese then add a layer of chives. Assemble the sandwich with the white bread in the center of the 2 brown slices. Cut off the crust and cut into 3 finger sandwiches.

Cheryl says this is *Beautiful and Yummy*!

Welsh Rabbit Fingers

"The Book of Afternoon Tea"
Lesley Mackley

1/2 lb. sharp Cheddar cheese
2 Tbsp. butter, softened
1 Tbsp. Worcestershire sauce
1 tsp. mustard powder
1 Tbsp. all-purpose flour
About 1/4 cup beer
4 slices whole-wheat bread

Preheat broiler. Into a bowl, shred cheese. Add butter, Worcestershire sauce, mustard powder, flour and enough beer to make a stiff paste.

Toast bread on both sides. Spread cheese mixture over one side of each slice of toast.

Broil until topping is cooked through and well browned. Dust with cayenne. Cut each slice of toast into 3 triangles. Garnish with bell pepper strips and parsley sprigs.

Makes 12

Scones, Desserts and Toppings

Apricot Bavarian Cream

"A Year of Teas at the Elmwood Inn"
Shelley and Bruce Richardson

1 package orange-flavored gelatin
1/4 cup sugar
1 cup apricot juice
1 cup crushed apricots, drained
1 tsp. almond extract
1 cup whipping cream

Dissolve gelatin in 1 cup of hot water. Add sugar and apricot juice. Chill until cold and syrupy. Add apricots and almond extract.

Whip cream until soft peaks form. Fold into gelatin mixture. Spoon into a large glass dish or individual sherbet glasses. Chill until firm.

Serves 8

Reprinted with permission.

Apricot Bread

"Myrtle's Tea House"
Ridgefield, Washington

1/2 cup dried apricots
1 cup water
1 egg, slightly beaten
1 cup sugar
2 Tbsp. butter, melted
2 cups flour
1 Tbsp. baking powder
1/2 tsp. salt
1/4 tsp. baking soda
1/4 cup water
1/2 cup orange juice
1 cup chopped walnuts

In saucepan combine apricots and water. Bring to a boil and boil for 5 minutes. Remove from heat and cover for 20 minutes. Drain and chop. Combine apricots, eggs, sugar and melted butter. Combine flour, baking powder, salt and baking soda. Add dry ingredients to wet ingredients just until combined. Stir in water and orange juice. Add nuts. Bake in loaf pan at 350° for 1 hour or until done. When it is done - cool, slice and serve with cream cheese.

Printed with permission.

Bakewell Tarts

Daughters of the British Empire
Lake Oswego, Oregon

Pastry of your choice equivalent to 2 pie crusts
Seedless raspberry jam
1 stick (4 oz.) unsalted butter, softened
2/3 cup sugar
2 large eggs
2 cups ground almond meal (available from Trader Joe's
or grind whole almonds to a fine meal in food processor)
Powdered sugar

Using 3" cutter, line nonstick muffin tins with pastry
(pastry will come about half way up the sides of the tins), dab
a little raspberry jam (about 1/2 tsp.) on the pastry (not too
much, as it will boil over).

Cream butter and sugars with mixer, then beat in the eggs
till fluffy, scraping down the sides of the bowl. Fold in ground
almonds with a spatula and spread 1 heaped tsp. of the mixture
(about the size of a walnut) on top of the jam, being sure to
cover all the jam.

Bake at 375° for about 20-25 minutes or until slightly
browned on top. Cool on a rack and dust with powdered sugar.
May be frozen after they have cooled down.

Printed with permission.

Banoffee Mess

"America's Best Tea Room Recipes"
Brewster Teapot at the Beechcroft Inn
Brewster, Massachusetts

1 cup heavy whipping cream, whipped
6 large meringues
3 bananas, peeled and sliced
6 Tbsp. toffee or caramel sauce
6 Tbsp. chopped hazelnuts, toasted (*)

In a large bowl, place whipped cream. Crumble meringues over whipped cream. Carefully fold in sliced bananas. Swirl in toffee or caramel sauce. Spoon mixture evenly into 6 dessert glasses. Top with toasted hazelnuts and serve immediately.

(*) To toast, place chopped hazelnuts in a single layer on a baking sheet. Bake at 350° for approximately 10 minutes or until hazelnuts are golden brown.

Printed with permission.

Blueberry Curd

"The Tea Table"
Bruce and Shelly Richardson
Elmwood Inn

4 cups fresh blueberries, slightly crushed
1/2 cup fresh lemon juice
1 cup sugar
4 eggs (beaten)
1/2 cup unsalted butter
1 Tbsp. lemon zest

In a heavy pan, combine berries, lemon juice, sugar and eggs. Stir constantly over medium heat until blueberries are very soft. Next, add pieces of butter and the zest slowly, stirring constantly over medium heat until mixture just starts to boil. Immediately remove from heat. Cool. Pour into a covered container and place in refrigeration until ready to use. Stir before serving.

Printed with permission: Elmwood Inn Fine Teas & Benjamin Press.
205 East Fourth Street, Perryville, KY. 40468, 859-332-2400, freear@msn.com
This book may be purchased by calling
800-765-2139

Champagne Jelly

"Deepwood Delights"
Janice Palmquist

4 cups sugar
1 cup white grape juice
1 cup Brut Champagne
1/4 tsp. citric acid
3 ounce pouch of liquid pectin

In a deep saucepan combine the sugar, grape juice, champagne and citric acid. Cook the mixture, stirring constantly, over medium high heat until it comes to a full boil that cannot be stirred down. Add the pectin and cook the mixture to a full boil, stirring constantly, and allow the mixture to boil for one minute. Remove the saucepan from the heat and skim off the foam. Ladle into jars and seal.

Reprinted with permission.

Cherry Nut Cake

Brambleberry Cottage & Tea Shoppe
Spokane, Washington

2 1/2 cups sifted self-rising flour
1 1/2 cups sugar
1/2 cup shortening
3/4 cup milk
1/4 cup maraschino cherry juice
1 tsp. vanilla
4 egg whites
1/3 cup maraschino cherries, finely chopped
1/2 cup walnuts, chopped

Sift flour and sugar. Chop in shortening. Combine milk and cherry juice and add 3/4 cup of the mixture with vanilla to the flour mixture. Mix well. Add remaining liquid and egg whites. Mix well. Add cherries and nuts blend. Bake in three 9" layer pans that have been greased and floured for 20 minutes at 375°. When toothpick comes out clean, cakes are done. Cool 5 minutes and remove from pan.

Mock Whipped Cream Cake Icing

5 Tbsp. flour
1 cup milk
1 cup sugar
1 cup butter
1 tsp. vanilla

Cook flour and milk until thickened, stirring constantly. Cool. Cream sugar, butter and vanilla then add to cooled flour mixture. Beat until spreadable consistency and no lumps remain.

This is a *beautiful* cake with *wonderful* flavor!

Chocolate Pecan Toffee Bars

"Tea Time"
Nancy Akmon

2 sticks butter (1/2 lb.)
3/4 cup light brown sugar
1/4 cup granulated sugar
1 egg yolk
2 cups flour
1 tsp. vanilla extract
1 large pkg. chocolate chips (12 oz.)
1 cup pecans, toasted and chopped

Preheat oven to 350°. Butter a 13 x 9 inch baking pan. Toast and chop the nuts and set aside. With an electric mixer at low speed, cream together the butter, brown sugar and granulated sugar. Add the egg yolk and vanilla extract. Beat well. Stir in the flour. Spread this mixture onto the buttered baking pan. Bake 25 minutes. Remove from oven. Sprinkle top with the chocolate chips. Return pan to the oven for 1 minute. Using a knife spread the melted chocolate evenly across the surface of the pan. Sprinkle with the chopped nuts. Cool completely and cut into squares.

Cream Roses

"Having Tea"
Tricia Foley

3 cups strawberries, hulled, washed and dried
1 tsp. (1/2 package) unflavored gelatin
1 cup heavy cream
Approximately 3 Tbsp. confectioners' sugar
16 tartlet shells

Puree the strawberries in a food processor. Sprinkle the gelatin on top and pour the puree into a saucepan. Stir gently over very low heat until the gelatin dissolves. Let the puree cool to lukewarm.

Combine the cream with 3 Tbsp. confectioners' sugar (use slightly more if berries are tart) and whip until the cream is very thick. Fold in the lukewarm strawberry puree. Pipe the mixture in the shape of a rose into the tartlet shells. (*) Put the tartlets in the refrigerator for at least 2 hours, until set. Store cream roses in the refrigerator; serve chilled.

(*) Practice on a bit of waxed paper first.

Yield: 16 tartlets

Date and Pumpkin Bread

"Cheryl's Cup of Tea"
Oregon City, Oregon

3 1/2 cups all-purpose flour
2 tsp. baking soda
1 1/2 tsp. salt
1 tsp. cinnamon
1 tsp. nutmeg
3 cups sugar
1 cup oil
4 large eggs, beaten
2/3 cup water
2 cups (1 1/2 lb. can) pumpkin
1 1/4 cups pecans, chopped
1 cup dates, chopped (can substitute raisins)

Combine all dry ingredients and mix well. Combine wet ingredients and mix into dry ingredients. Add pecans and dates. Pour into 3 small greased loaf pans. Bake for 1 hour. Allow to set several hours before slicing.

Cheryl says that these mini loaves are fragrant with spices and make great hostess gifts.

Earl Grey Crème Bruleé

"The Great Tea Rooms of America"
Bruce and Shelley Richardson
Elmwood Inn

1 1/2 quarts heavy cream
5 whole large eggs, slightly beaten
5 large egg yolks, slightly beaten
1 1/2 cups brown sugar
1 cup white sugar
1 cup Earl Grey tea, strongly brewed

Preheat oven to 350°. Place heavy cream, slightly beaten eggs, egg yolks and sugars in the top of double boiler. Cook over medium heat, stirring frequently until slightly thickened. Add tea and pour into small ramekins. Bake until set, approximately 50-60 minutes. Custard is done when knife stuck in center comes out clean. Cool to room temperature and refrigerate overnight.

Mix a small amount of brown sugar and white sugar together. Pat lightly on top of custard and then torch until sugar melts. Serve immediately.

Printed with permission; Elmwood Inn Fine Teas & Benjamin Press,
205 East Fourth Street, Perryville, KY 40468, 859-332-2400, freear@msn.com

This book may be ordered by calling
800-765-2139

Eton Chaos

"The Tea Experience"
from Teatime Magazine

2 egg whites
1/4 tsp. cream of tartar
1/2 cup sugar
2 cups heavy whipping cream
1/3 cup confectioners sugar
2 cups chopped strawberries
Garnish: fresh mint sprigs, strawberries

Preheat oven to 225°. Line baking sheet with parchment paper. In medium bowl and using electric mixer at high speed, beat egg whites to stiff peaks. Add cream of tartar; gradually beat in sugar. Drop meringues into egg-sized mounds onto prepared baking sheet. Bake 2 1/2 hours.

In medium bowl and using electric mixer at medium speed, beat cream cheese until soft peaks form. Crumble meringues into chips. Combine cream, strawberries and meringue chips. Garnish with fresh mint and strawberries, if desired.

Meringues can be made up to a week ahead and stored in airtight containers.

Makes 6-8 servings

Green Tea Ice Cream

"The Tea and Herb Shop"
Corvallis, Oregon

1 pint vanilla ice cream
1 tsp. Matcha

Peggy uses Ben and Jerry's organic ice cream and the second grade Matcha which is organic.

Soften the ice cream, blend in green tea powder and chill. Serve and enjoy!

Hannah Marie Country Scones

"Tea Time at the Inn"
Gail Greco

3 cups all-purpose flour
2 Tbsp. baking powder
1/2 tsp. baking soda
1 1/2 Tbsp. sugar
2 sticks ice-cold butter, cut into 1-inch slices
2 cups buttermilk
Buttermilk

Combine flour, baking powder, baking soda and sugar with a fork. Using a pastry cutter, cut butter into dry mixture. Chill for 10 minutes; preheat oven to 400°. Add 2 cups buttermilk, mixing until all ingredients are moistened. Gather into a ball and knead about 12 times. Roll out pastry to 1-inch thickness. Cut scones with a 2-inch biscuit cutter. Place on an ungreased baking sheet, close together, but not touching. Brush tops with remaining buttermilk. Bake for 20 minutes or until golden brown. Serve hot.

Yield: 12

Lavender Butter

"Tea Party"
Tracy Stern with Christie Matheson

1 stick (1/2 cup) unsalted butter, softened
1 Tbsp. lemon juice
1 Tbsp. finely chopped fresh chives
1 tsp. ground dried lavender flowers
1/4 tsp. salt
1/4 tsp. white pepper

Using a fork, combine butter, lemon juice, chives, lavender, salt and pepper in bowl. Spoon the mixture into two clean glass votive holders or small ramekins and refrigerate for at least 1 hour or up to a day. If you refrigerate it for longer than 1 hour, let it soften at room temperature for 15 minutes before serving.

Makes about 1/2 cup

Lazy Peach Pie

"An Afternoon to Remember"
Newcastle, California

1/2 cup butter
1 cup sugar
1 cup flour
2 tsp. baking powder
3/4 cup milk
1 large can of sliced peaches

Preheat oven to 350°. Place butter in 9 x 13 pan and melt in oven while it is preheating. Take out when melted. Sift sugar, flour and baking powder. Mix the sifted ingredients with the milk. Pour the mixture over the melted butter in the pan.

Pour the can of peaches (not drained) over the batter. Do not mix.

Sprinkle cinnamon and sugar over the top.

Bake at 350° for 1 hour.

Lemon Bar Delite

"Steeped in Comfort"
Lakewood, Washington

1/2 cup butter
1 cup flour
1/2 cup powdered sugar

Crumb above ingredients. Bake 15 minutes at 350°

Mix together the following:
1 cup sugar
2 Tbsp. lemon juice
2 eggs beaten
2 Tbsp. flour
1/2 tsp. baking powder
Grated rind from 1 lemon

Pour over 1st mixture after it is cooled.

Bake in 8 x 8 pan for 25 minutes at 350°

Frost with powdered sugar frosting made from:
11/2 tsp. lemon juice
1/2 tsp. vanilla
3/4 cup powdered sugar
1 Tbsp. butter

Cut into 2 x 2 squares.
Double recipe for 9 x 13 pan to make 32 squares.

Lemon Cream Scones

"Tea Time"
Nancy Akmon

2 cups unbleached flour
1/3 cup sugar
1 Tbsp. baking powder
1/4 tsp. salt
1/2 cup golden raisins
1 tsp. lemon peel, grated fine
1 cup whipping cream
3 Tbsp. water
1 egg, beaten

Preheat oven to 375°. In a large mixing bowl, add the flour, sugar, baking powder and salt. Stir in the raisins and lemon zest. Slowly stir in the cream to the bowl and the 3 Tbsp. water. Using a fork, continue to stir *just* until the dough is formed. Turn out the dough onto a lightly floured bread board and knead the dough for a minute. Place the dough onto a greased baking sheet. Lightly press the dough with your hands to form an 8 inch circle. With a knife, that has been dipped in flour, cut almost all the way through the dough into 12 wedges as in a pie. Brush tops with the beaten egg. Bake for 25-30 minutes.

Lemon Meringue

"A Touch of Elegance"
Saint John's, Washington

3/4 stick (6 Tbsp.) unsalted butter
1 Tbsp. fresh lemon zest
2 cups fresh lemon juice
1/2 cup sugar
3 large eggs and 2 egg yolks

Melt butter. Add sugar, lemon juice and lemon zest, stirring until sugar is dissolved. Whisk eggs together and whisk in lemon mixture until combined well. Transfer curd to pan and heat over medium heat, whisking constantly until it just begins to simmer. Pour curd through a fine sieve into a bowl and cool slightly. Chill at least 2 hours or until cold or up to 3 days.

No-Fuss Chocolate Squares

"Breakfast at Nine, Tea at Four"
Sue Carroll

1 1/2 cups finely crushed graham cracker crumbs
1 (14 oz.) can sweetened condensed milk
1 cup semisweet chocolate chips (6 oz.)
1/2 cup chopped walnuts
1/2 tsp. salt

Preheat the oven to 350°. Grease well a 9 inch square baking pan. Combine all ingredients in a large bowl. Mix until well blended. Spread evenly in the prepared pan and bake for 20 minutes or until lightly browned. Cool on a rack and cut into squares.

Yield: 24 squares

Orange Cranberry Tea Scones

A La Fontaine
Albany, Oregon

3 cup Spelt, whole wheat, white or combination flour
1/3 cup organic cane sugar
2 1/2 tsp. baking powder
1/2 tsp. salt
1/2 tsp. soda
1 stick butter
1 cup buttermilk
3/4 cup dried cranberries
2 tsp. orange or grapefruit zest

In a large bowl, stir flour, sugar, baking powder, and salt. Add pieces of butter and beat with electric mixer until well blended. Add cranberries and zest. Pour in buttermilk and mix until blended. Divide dough in 1/2, gather into balls and roll each ball into 2 circles, 3/4" thick. Cut each ball into 8 wedges.

Bake 12-15 minutes in preheated 400° oven on lightly greased pans. Remove from oven and brush with glaze.

Glaze

Combine 2 Tbsp. cream, 1/4 tsp. ground cinnamon and 4 Tbsp. granulated sugar.

Reprinted with permission.

Orange Iced Cranberry Cookies

"Cheryl's Cup of Tea"
Oregon City, Oregon

3/4 cup sugar
1/2 cup brown sugar
1/2 cup butter, softened
1/2 cup sour cream
1 tsp. vanilla
2 eggs
2 1/4 cups all purpose flour
1/2 tsp. baking soda
1/2 tsp. baking powder
1 cup fresh cranberries, chopped
1/2 cup walnuts, chopped

Preheat oven to 350°. In a large mixing bowl, combine sugars, butter, sour cream, vanilla and eggs. Blend well. Add flour, baking soda and baking powder; gently stir in the cranberries and nuts. Do not over-mix. Drop by teaspoon full 2" apart on lightly greased cookie sheets. Bake 11 to 13 minutes or until golden brown. Let cool; frost with icing.

Icing

2 cups powdered sugar
2 Tbsp. margarine or butter, melted
1 tsp. grated orange peel zest
1-3 Tbsp. orange juice

In a small mixing bowl, blend all ingredients and spread on cooled cookies. Cheryl shared that these are wonderful for the holidays.

Yield: 5 dozen

Pecan Coconut Scones

"Cheryl's Treasured Tea Time"
Sacramento, California

10 Tbsp. butter
2 eggs
1 cup buttermilk
1 Tbsp. coconut extract or syrup

1 Tbsp. plus 1 tsp. baking powder
5 Tbsp. sugar
4 cups sugar
finely chopped pecans
finely chopped coconut
finely chopped white chocolate

In mixer combine first four ingredients and blend. When blended, slowly add the dry ingredients in the order given. Mix until batter pulls away from the side of the bowl. Roll out on floured surface (minimum kneading and handling of dough). Cut out desired shapes at about 1/2" thickness. Brush top with egg whites and bake in convection oven at 325° for 20-25 minutes. In conventional oven, bake at 375° for 20 minutes and check the bottoms to make sure they are finished.

Makes 14 medium scones

Pumpkin Walnut Bars

"Ms. Lynn's Tea Table and More"
Carol Perlick

4 eggs
1 2/3 cup sugar
1 cup oil
1-16 oz. can pumpkin
2 cups flour
1 tsp. baking powder
2 tsp. cinnamon
1 tsp. salt
1 tsp. baking soda

In a large mixing bowl combine eggs, sugar and pumpkin, beating until light and fluffy. Stir dry ingredients together and slowly add to egg mixture. Continue beating until smooth. Pour into UN-GREASED jelly roll pan. Bake at 350° for 25-30 minutes.

Frosting

6 oz. cream cheese, softened
1/2 cup butter, softened
2 tsp. vanilla
2 cups powdered sugar

Beat butter and cream cheese; add vanilla and powdered sugar. A few drops of milk may be necessary to thin mixture for spreading consistency. Freezes well.

Rum Cakes

"Ms. Lynn's Tea Table and More"
Carol Perlick

4 eggs
1/2 cup oil
1/2 cup water
1/2 cup white rum
1 small box instant vanilla pudding
1 box yellow cake mix

Mix together and pour into greased and flowered pans (shaped fluted pans, bundt or mini bundt pans). Bake at 350° for 40 to 50 minutes. After taking the cake out of the oven, pour hot sauce (below) over it while still in the pans.

Sauce

1 cup sugar
1 cup butter
1/2 cup rum (white)
1/2 cup water

Boil mixture for 1 to 2 minutes, and then pour over warm cakes.

Makes 12

Reprinted with permission.

Sydney Custard Tart

"The ANZAC Tea Parlour"
The Dalles, Oregon

4 egg yolks
1/2 cup sugar
2 Tbsp. corn starch
3/4 cup heavy cream
1/2 cup water
1 strip lemon rind
2 tsp. vanilla essence
1 sheet rolled puff pastry

Preheat oven to 425°. Whisk egg yolks, sugar, and corn starch in medium saucepan until combined. Gradually whisk in cream and water until smooth. Add lemon rind strip. Stir over medium heat until mixture boils and thickens. Remove pan from heat. Remove and discard lemon rind. Stir in vanilla and cover surface of custard with plastic wrap. Let cool.

Grease muffin or tart pan. Cut puff pastry into circles and press into muffin pan with your fingers. Spoon cooled custard into pastry. Bake in hot oven for 20 minutes or until well browned. Let cool for 5 minutes.

Index

Tea Rooms Index-Oregon
Alphabetical Listing
(City Listing on page 215)

Tea Rooms Index-Oregon
Alphabetical Listing
(City Listing on page 215)

Tea Rooms Index-Washington

Alphabetical Listing

(City Listing on page 218)

Tea Rooms Index-Washington
Alphabetical Listing
(City Listing on page 218)

Tea Rooms Index-Northern California

Alphabetical Listing

(City Listing on page 220)

Tea Rooms Index-Oregon
City Listing
(Alphabetical Listing on page 210)

Tea Rooms Index-Oregon

City Listing

(Alphabetical Listing on page 210)

Tea Rooms Index-Oregon

City Listing

(Alphabetical Listing on page 210)

Tea Rooms Index-Washington

City Listing
(Alphabetical Listing on page 212)

Tea Rooms Index-Washington
City Listing
(Alphabetical Listing on page 212)

Tea Rooms Index-Northern California

City Listing

(*Alphabetical Listing on page 214*)

Tea Rooms Index-Northern California
City Listing
(Alphabetical Listing on page 214)

Recipes Index

Beverages

Sandwiches, Savories, Salads and Soups

Recipes Index

Scones, Desserts & Toppings

Be a TEA ROOM Spotter

When you're out-and-about and discover a new tea spot, please let us know. Many of our best new "finds" come from tea spotters like you. *Thank you for sharing.*

How to Report a New Tea Room

You can email the information to us at: TeaRoomsNorthwest@hotmail.com. If you prefer to mail it in, send the information requested below with the tea rooms business card, and a flyer if possible, to:

Tea Rooms Northwest Staff
2397 N.W. Kings Blvd. # 148
Corvallis, Oregon 97330

Tea Room Name:_____

Contact Person:_____

Address:_____

City:_____

State/Province/Zip:_____

Phone:_____

Referred by:_____

Address:_____

City:_____

State/Province/Zip:_____

Is Journaling for You?

Journaling is a wonderful, lasting keepsake of your time spent with family and friends enjoying a tea-time experience. Keeping a journal can nurture your sentimental side and feed the desire to capture special moments in your life.

If you are smitten by the tea experience as we are, or you have "Tea Room" memories you would like to save, then journaling is for you. Our mission is to promote your tea room experience as much as possible!

The *TEA TIME JOURNAL* is a unique journal and measures 8½" x 5½." The 80 page book features space to journal 30 tea room visits. You can record your observations on the menus, presentations, service, with room for pictures. The *TEATIME JOURNAL* includes a tea glossary, trivia, tea facts, our favorite scone recipe, a tea quiz, and plenty of room for your thoughts and inspirations. The *TEA TIME JOURNAL* is the perfect gift for all tea lovers.

See next page for ordering information.

A Tea Time Journal
is the perfect gift for
tea lovers everywhere

To order copies of the
TEA TIME JOURNAL, please
provide us with the information listed
below or make a photocopy of this page.
Send your order along with a
check or money order
in the amount of $9.95 USD
for each book and $2 for S&H

J&S Publishing
2397 N.W. Kings Blvd. # 148
Corvallis, Oregon 97330 USA

If you prefer to pay by credit card,
you may do so on the web at:
www.paypal.com
and send payment to: demontigny@proaxis.com

Name: _____

Address: _____

City: _____

State/Providence/Zip: _____

You may also contact us at:
TeaRoomsNorthwest@hotmail.com

Tea Rooms Northwest

Your Guide to Tea Rooms,
Tea Events and Tea Time Recipes

This book takes you on a journey through Northwest
tea rooms with a vivid description of the atmosphere
and foods at tea rooms in Oregon,
Washington, and Northern California.

We invite you to take this book in hand and visit
the many outstanding tearooms the
Northwest has to offer.

For more information you can email us at:
TeaRoomNorthwest@hotmail.com

$19.95 USD for each book plus $4 S&H

J&S Publishing

2397 N.W. Kings Blvd. # 148
Corvallis, Oregon 97330 USA

If you prefer to pay by credit card,
you may do so on the web at:
www.paypal.com
and send payment to: demontigny@proaxis.com

Name: _____

Address: _____

City: _____

State/Providence/Zip: _____

For wholesale information contact us at:
TeaRoomsNorthwest@hotmail.com

Tea Room Discoveries

Tea Room Discoveries

Tea Room Discoveries